SOUNDTRACKS OF MY LIFE

© Carl Cleves 2022

Carl Cleves has asserted his right to be identified as Author of this work

Photographs are from the author's personal collection.
Cover art images created by Carl Cleves with Midjourney.

All rights reserved. No part of this publication may be reproduced or transmitted in any form or by any means, electronic or mechanical, including photocopying, recording, or any information storage or retrieval, without prior permission in writing from the author.

ISBN 978-0-6451360-1-2

SOUNDTRACKS OF MY LIFE

Carl Cleves

ALSO BY CARL CLEVES

Tarab – Travels with my guitar
Dancing with the Bones

*For Calliope and Apollo,
Saraswati and Oshun
And all their devotees,
music aficionados*

'Without music,
life would be a mistake.'

- Friedrich Nietzsche

CONTENTS

	PARTY AT MY HOUSE	9
1	MY FAVOURITE CHANNEL	13
2	HENRI SALVADOR	17
3	SKIFFLE	27
4	LES CHANSONNIERS	33
5	LONNIE JOHNSON	45
6	ROCK&ROLL	55
7	JESSE FULLER	67
8	FOLK	71
9	AFRICA	83
10	HIPPIES AND REFUGEES	95
11	INDIA	99
12	ROBBIE BASHO	111
13	DOLLAR BRAND	119
14	KEITH JARRETT	123
15	BRAZIL	131
16	WORLD MUSIC	149
17	THE QUEEN OF MALAGASY MUSIC	155
18	VAZAHA AND VEZO	191
19	THE MAN IN THE LIME-GREEN SUIT/ TARAB IN MAJUNGA	203
20	A DESERT ISLAND COLLECTION	213
	MADAGASCAR GLOSSARY	245
	ABOUT CARL CLEVES	248
	TARAB. TRAVELS WITH MY GUITAR	251
	DANCING WITH THE BONES	253
	DISCOGRAPHY	255
	REVIEWS	256

PARTY AT MY HOUSE

When I was just a little baby
I already was a-rockin' in my cradle
Mama said: "look at that crazy kid.
Oh no! We haven't seen the end of it.
Can't keep that boy from going off!"
Can't keep that boy from going off!
Come join the party at my house

Brother Luc and cousin Kate
Well, they stayed home to procreate
But I lost my cool and burned the treaty
When Jacques Brel left for Tahiti
Soon I strayed from place to place
With a steel string guitar in its case
And my pack on my back
With a map on the track
All night boogie at the chicken shack
Come join the party at my house

Big Bill Broonzy slammin' on the guitar
Bill Black's combo picking out the bass line
The one and only mister Macaroni
Blows fire from a saxophone
Look at them women jiving on the dance floor
Waiting for you to come messing with the décor

You start shakin' 'till you can't take no more
Are you ready? One two three four
Come join the party at my house

I climb the roof and raise my flag
When Papa brings his brand new bag
Easy skanking, I am dancing
On that Rasta man I'm banking

The pharaoh in Egypt plucked his lyre
While the mummies set the crypt on fire!
From the Delta to Chicago
Muddy Waters worked his mojo
But now the kids don't care for blues
They wanna dance with hip hop shoes
Western Swing and Country, oh no!
All we want is doof and techno!
Come join the party at my house

Nat King Cole and Rock my Soul
Feel like I'm knocking on heaven's door
I just can't control my feet
I'm on heat with the beat

Xango, Exu, Yemanja
Were the mighty Orixa
Who travelled from Nigeria
To Cuba, Haiti, Jamaica
For many years they kept it hidden
In sacred drums that secret rhythm

So if you're tired of doing waltzes
Dance the mambo, rumba, salsa
Come join the party at my house

I walk the beach in Honolulu
I'm in a bar room in Hong Kong
Not for long you come along
And ask me for a Hottentot song
Mabo, Cravo and Zimbabwe
Dim Dim, you will go A Long Way
Come join the party at my house

If you're feeling sore and stiff
You don't have to burn a spliff
All you need is an afro riff
Mbaqanga, Pachanga
Pop-Makossa, Kwasa Kwasa
Jit, Juju, Fuji and Marabi
Pachanga, Mbaqanga,
Makossa, Kwasa Kwasa
Jit, Juju, Fuji and Marabi

Baaba Maal, Fela Kuti,
Youssou, Franco and Salif,
Tabu Ley, Sam Mangwana,
Papa Wemba, Jimmy Cliff
Benga, Chimurenga,
Kalindula, Marrabenta
Benga, Chimurenga,
Kalindula, Marrabenta

Baaba Maal, Toure Kounda,
Pepe Kale and Salif,
Tabu Ley, Chico Cesar,
Tina Turner, Jimmy Cliff
Benga, Chimurenga,
Kalindula, Marrabenta
Benga, Chimurenga,
Kalindula, Marrabenta
Come join the party at my house

Cop. Carl Cleves
(from The Hottentots album *Turn Back The Tide*)

1

MY FAVOURITE CHANNEL

This afternoon I ambled through the bustling centre of my home town, Byron Bay. How the town has changed. It was a sleepy and forgotten village on the most easterly edge of the Australian continent when Parissa and I first landed here to sing African and Bulgarian songs along the thumping waves, and to romance in the shallow, tea tree soaked waters of Belongil creek. Only surfers and hippies knew the secret beauty of this hamlet that had survived cedar tree logging and sand mining, had witnessed the hacking of bloody carcasses of whales, then cattle, dumping their offal into the mother of all oceans, sending a foul stench adrift over the beaches, a feast for sharks. In the lush green hinterland and the volcanic soil of the valleys farmers grew sugar cane, milked cows and traded butter. Who could have guessed then that, years later, Parissa and I would build a house at the edge of the Belongil creek wetlands, where I now sit typing these words at my open window? Summer cicadas cackle in code. A dazzle of bats sweeps across the dark cerulean sky. Beyond the hidden forest the Pacific Ocean babbles: 'tonight all is good with the world.'

Since then Byron central has become a tourist mecca in the Lonely Planet guide. Whales are watched, not harpooned. Funky homegrown stores have been replaced by the big outlets selling women's fashion and surfboards. No longer can I buy a toaster. Music blares out of every shop and bar, buskers are amplified. But come follow me, just out of town, into my backyard where the sky remains tuned to bird song and the sea breeze whispers in the Bangalow palms, my favourite channel for lying in the hammock, pondering the soundtracks of my life, travelling back on the silver wheels of the Pacific Ocean, with eyes closed and my ears open to the past. My song lines have been stretched like a spider's web by

> A lyre player in Uganda
> An oud player in Khartoum
> A bearded cantor in an orthodox church in Corfu
> A Senegalese griot who came to my hut in Casamance
> to play his kora in the dark
> The pigmy yodelling of my wife bewitching me night after
> night on endless tours
> Champion Jack Dupree in a night club in Brussels
> Egberto Gismonti at a free concert in a park in
> Belo Horizonte
> A tempestuous piano player from Ferriday, Louisiana
> A spectacled rockabilly star who died in a plane crash
> A blind child's singing and clapping hands on a
> train in Bihar
> Kirtans for Guru Nanak in a Sikh gurdwara
> Trumpets, gongs and the conch shells of Tibetan monks
> in Kalimpong

The trance inducing chants of an Antandroy family
in Tulear, Madagascar
An Afro-rumba dance band on a hot Nairobi night
An indigenous group from Arnhem Land at a festival
in Alice Springs
A Tamoure troupe in a seaside joint in Papeete on
New Year's eve
An all-night exorcism to cure a village
in Bahia from a scourge of conjunctivitis
Jacques Brel singing 'Le Plat Pays' on a juke box
in a student bar in Leuven

These experiences have remained as deeply carved into my memory banks as has the birth of my son, meeting my wife, or my various near death episodes. I would like to share of few of them with you.

2

HENRI SALVADOR

Mynah birds, honeyeaters and drongos plunged in turn into the bird bath, diving, dipping and ducking, flapping their wings, splashing water, dashing off to let others swoop from the waiting bushes to secure a spot. Parissa, Andreina and I were lounging on the back veranda, enjoying the last of the Friday afternoon. Bellbirds tinkled their tiny chimes. A short walk from here, beyond a forest of paperbark trees, palms and figs, shrubs and tough grasses, the mighty ocean murmured, napping under the searing, setting sun. The wind had dropped and the tide was ebbing. Soon the cicadas, crickets, frogs and bats, creatures of the tropical night, would revamp the soundscape. We were idly teasing each other, gossiping and reminiscing about our childhoods, digging down into our memories to solve a riddle. What was the first song, that first musical thrill of our infancy, that opened our ears to the magic mystery of music? All three of us are musicians. We mark our path by musical milestones. Parissa was the first to serenade us with 'Shimmy Shimmy Ko Ko Bop', a catchy nonsense song stranded in her brain's playlist since forever. Her very first earworm.

'And then I proudly went to my mum to play her my first composition on my toy piano,' she recalled. It was 'God Save the Queen'. She was too young to discern the difference between learning and composing a tune.

Andreina, who had been sitting there with her eyes closed, burst into a cumbia dance hit she had duetted, snuggled with her mother, careening in a hammock in their Caracas home in Venezuela.

And all I could hear was Henri Salvador singing 'Maladie d' amour'.

My childhood home in Mechelen, Belgium was not generously blessed with music. A mundane radio offered news bulletins while the family sat down for lunch, classical music in the morning, then some popular songs in French, Dutch, German, Italian and, increasingly, in English as we moved into the 1950s. School offered Gregorian chants and a choir that focused on a classical repertoire. I did not see any live performances as a child. Music was for adults, or for dedicated conservatorium alumni practicing scales and reading scores. So when my aural spectrum suddenly lit up and sent my heart racing I was taken by surprise.

'Maladie d' amour.'

I don't recall exactly when I first noticed the song, but have learned since that it hit the parade in 1948. I was five years old then and its beguiling swing has remained with me. Every time I hear it, it sounds like the first time. 'Maladie d' amour' was one of the tunes I would sing for my brother Eric at night, when we still shared a bed and played radio games, hidden under the blankets so that my parents would not hear us. The song was in creole French, but there was enough there to catch on to and sing along with the chorus: maladie d'amour, maladie des amoureux, maladie de la jeunesse. It had the sweetness of a lullaby on a warm night, the charm and the spell of young love.

The record opened with a mystery ploy. Church bells tolled. Birds warbled. And you imagined a small village on a sultry day, coconut palm trees swaying in the sea breeze until, all of a sudden, Henri's guitar strummed such an effortless swinging chacha that it ensnarled you while his smooth voice crooned:

> Maladi damour
> Maladi dé zamoureu
> Chacha si'w enmen-mwen
> Wa maché dèyè-mwen
> Maladi damour
> Maladi de la jeunes

The song was irresistible. As soon as it was over, you wanted to hear it again. Much later I saw him on TV, mimicking the chimes by striking the strings while whirling his guitar from side to side, whistling the chirping of birds, until he burst into the song like a magician who pulls a rabbit from a hat. The malady of love was my initiation into the sensual sound and stirring rhythm of the tropics, the call of the clear blue light of the Southern Hemisphere where I would spend most of my life. It promised me that everything that was lacking in the Gothic caverns of my childhood, existed. The freedom to fly above the cloud cover of rigid taboos and regulations was yours to choose.

Henri Salvador would remain on the soundtrack of my youth. His voice could instantly veer from a rambunctious and contagious guffaw to a croon, seductive like a sweet liqueur, so luscious and enticing that it would make any woman -and most men- swoon. Coffee and cream elegance in a white suit, cropped creole hair leaving his face a canvas for his mimicry, dark cheeky eyes and a grin that opened wide like an accordion. He became a big star on the pop charts and in the movies and did hilarious comedy skits on TV. He was part of the furniture, as familiar as the large painting that overlooked our dining room table of a blonde woman with a straw hat, a summer dress and a bouquet of flowers, seated on the back of an elephant in a golden field of ripe wheat, a church steeple and a windmill in the distance and a boy turning his back to piss against a tree stump.

When I left Europe soundtracks morphed with the weather and the mileage until, decades later, Salvador suddenly reappeared on my radar while I was living in Belo Horizonte, the capital of the Brazilian state of Minas Gerais. Intrigued, I began to take an interest in the man behind the song and discovered his extraordinary trajectory. Let me share it with you.

Henri was born in Cayenne, the capital of French Guyana, the notorious penal colony, famous for the book and the film Papillon and the fourteen long years of escapes from its hellhole by another Henri, Henri Charrière. Henri Salvador's father, Clovis, and his mother, Antonine, daughter of a native Carib Indian, were both from Guadeloupe in the French West Indies. In 1929 the Salvador family left Guyana, disembarking in the French port of Le Havre. Henri was twelve years old but, already on the trip across the Atlantic, his talents and clownery had been on display to the passengers. He was a natural. To the dismay of his father, he soon abandoned his studies, instead learning the instruments his father played – the trumpet and the violin—as well as the ones he took a shine to, the guitar and the drums. Around that time one, of his cousins played him records by Louis Armstrong and Duke Ellington and Henri was hooked. He listened and he learned. All day long. He blossomed. Django Reinhardt was king in France and Henri copied, to play like him. Before long, his talents were noticed, so much so that Django Reinhardt himself employed him as an accompanist. But the family had arrived in Europe at an uncertain time. Countries were boosting their military readiness. By the mid-thirties another world war loomed.

Henri was eighteen and called up for military service in the French army. Military discipline! Racist abuse! He deserted, was caught and imprisoned and, after serving his sentence, sent to the Northern Front where the Germans were crushing the French army. He managed to scrape back to Paris, but soon fled the occupied city for the free south where he found work as a singer and guitarist in Nice and Cannes. His fine-tuned choreographed performances disguised a brilliant musicianship and caught the eye of Ray Ventura who invited him to join his orchestra. Henri was twenty-four.

And thus a new chapter started in the life of young Henri Salvador. The Ventura orchestra left occupied Europe for South America where they toured Argentina, Uruguay and Brazil during the remaining years of the war. His contribution to the shows as a guitarist, singer and comedian made him a hit with Latin audiences and, when Ventura returned to France, Henri remained in Brazil for a solo tour. It was the continent of his childhood. From creole West Indian carnival songs and Django's gypsy jazz, he now adopted the samba, slowing it down to plant the first seeds of the coming craze: the bossa nova.

Salvador was such an arresting talent that he would have made it anywhere. Returning to France after the war he scored his first big hit with the song that gave me my childhood thrill and made him a star. 'Maladie d'amour' was a carnival song of days gone by, a beguine of Martinique, satirical as carnival songs often are. It made fun of an older woman, named Chacha, who loved younger boys. After its first recording seventeen years earlier it had entered West Indian folklore, but Henri had put his stamp on it. Though many covers followed, from the Ames Brothers, Dean Martin, the Cameroonian sax player Manu Dibango to a Mexican rock band, it is Salvador's version that remains unforgettable.

After his first hit his career exploded. He acted in films, was the host on popular French TV shows, had success with comedy songs and sugary sweet ballads and, from the sixties on, with the first French rock songs, including versions of 'The Twist', 'The Lion Sleeps Tonight' and 'Zorro est arrivé', which was adapted from The Coasters' 'Along Came Jones'. Ironically, despite these hits, he always claimed that he disliked rock and roll. By then I had gone off Henri Salvador. My childhood hero had sold out. He was a fake! As a teenager I hated these opportunistic records that I had to suffer daily on the radio. 'Juanita Banana' was perhaps an inspired novelty song, but his zany soap opera hysteria became grating in 1966, the year Dylan's Blonde on Blonde, The Stones' '19th Nervous Breakdown' and the Beatles' 'Paperback Writer' came out. I saw Henri as uncool, a bourgeois nerd on prime time TV who had peddled his soul for fame.

Wandering the musical path is a lifelong journey of discovery, as a listener, a performer or as a composer. In 1981 it was my turn to arrive in Brazil. In my teenage years I had fallen under the spell of Brazilian guitarists, but now my taste broadened and my ears stretched. Whereas the view from outside is always like peeping at the night sky through a crack in a wall, embedding in another culture reveals a whole new galaxy. And so I rediscovered Henri Salvador in Brazil through a recording of one of its finest songwriters, Caetano Veloso, who had covered Henri's 1957 hit 'Dans mon île', a sensual and seductive aquarelle of a personal island where one lazes about under the palm trees, basking in the sun, no thoughts of tomorrow, nothing to do but caress 'ma doudou', my sweetheart. An archetypal song. It encapsulated the sensual laid-back essence of Brazil, everyone's dream, the perfect escape fantasy. And suddenly the man, who I had regarded as a traitor, who had never fulfilled what he had promised when singing 'Maladie d'amour', took me by surprise again and I had to reassess the childhood hero I had dismissed.

Brazilians, whose hearts he had captured in 1945, knew him as the artist who influenced Antônio Carlos Jobim in siring the bossa nova. They adored him. Indeed, in 2005, three years before Henri's death, Gilberto Gil, the popular singer and songwriter who became Minister of Culture, presented Henri Salvador, in the presence of President Luiz Inácio Lula da Silva, with the Brazilian Order of Cultural Merit for his influence on Brazilian culture, particularly on bossa nova, to whose invention he contributed.

In France and Europe his career faded during the eighties and nineties. He made voice-overs in movies and appeared on TV shows, but for me he was out of range. Until, at the start of the millennium, his chocolate voice seduced me once more with a lilting bossa song, 'Jardin d'hiver'. He recorded his final album, Reverence, in 2006. He turned 87. Both Caetano Veloso and Gilberto Gil, the iconic Brazilian superstars of whom I will write more, joined him in the studio.

Three years later the great Henri Salvador, my first muse, left us. I never tried to find out much about his personal life, but he had flair, possessed a rare gift. He was the quintessential entertainer. That was enough. The many-facetted artist, musician, clown and vaudeville actor, helped us dream. He made us laugh. He made us feel good. I invite you into my dreams, Henri. Come and see me some time.

3

SKIFFLE

In the summer of 1957 I travelled with my neighbourhood Boy Scouts group to Birmingham in England to participate in the Ninth World Scout Jamboree. I had just turned fourteen and had already spent years with the Scouts. I loved the camps in the forests of the Ardennes and felt at home in the outdoors, being taught different things—like to recognise the leaves of birch, oak, poplar trees and beeches; to build an emergency forest shelter and a fire place for cooking; to huddle around a camp fire at night and look up at the Milky Way; to squat in the wet grass at dawn, spellbound and rooted, espying a family of deer, nibbling on grasses and wild flowers, antlers and heads down, steam vaporising from their nostrils. Our troupe was called the *Woudlopers* (Wood Runners) and our leaders were ex-army para-commandos, the Belgian special forces of that time, tough guys who taught us how to build hang bridges across streams and made us navigate rafts built from oil drums in the middle of winter. I adored it. But the Jamboree would signal my final days as a Scout.

Thirty-three thousand Boy Scouts from eighty-five countries were camped out in a park in Sutton Coldfield, outside of Birmingham. An additional seventeen thousand British Scouts had pitched their tents on sites nearby and another seven thousand boys were being bussed in from all over England for day visits. For twelve days I would be living in a tent city of boys, tackling unfamiliar words, befriending kids from Trinidad and India, from Liverpool and Nairobi. Before that I had only crossed the Belgian border for holidays with my parents to the south coast of France. The Jamboree made me an internationalist. All that boy energy could have launched a satellite. Together we celebrated the one hundred years since the birth of our founder Baden-Powell. There was a constant buzz with mass events and variety shows. On the second night I caught an enduring virus that had broken out around the camp city. It was called skiffle. A trio of exuberant Scouts stood outside their tent banging a guitar, scrubbing a washboard and thumping a tea-chest bass at a furious pace, singing 'John Henry was a steel driving man' and 'Digging my Potatoes', surrounded by a captive crowd of ebullient boys. It made my heart beat faster and triggered my teenage growth hormones.

Unbeknownst to me then, an Englishman named Lonnie Donegan had a Top Ten hit with an American folk-blues song first recorded in 1934 by John Lomax, as sung by inmates in an Arkansas State Prison. Leadbelly had popularised it. The song was 'Rock Island Line'. It went gold and Lonnie became the 'King of Skiffle'. Dixieland Trad Jazz had been the latest craze in England, leaving the swing period of jazz behind. Lonnie played guitar and sang with such an ensemble, the Chris Barber band. With two other band mates on bass and washboard, Lonnie began to play what the posters called 'skiffle breaks' of rousing versions of old Leadbelly, Woody Guthrie and American traditional tunes. The sound rapidly caught on.

Skiffle had originated in the American South between the two world wars with down-home jug bands scouring a washboard, plucking a washtub bass, strumming a guitar or frailing a banjo, buzzing the mouth of the jug or a stovepipe, trumpeting a kazoo, rattling the spoons, twanging the jaw harp or bowing the saw. Whatever was at hand. The bands played lively, unsophisticated tunes such as 'Skiffle Blues', 'Stealin', 'Walk right in' and 'On The road again', up-tempo jazz, blues and suggestive hokum songs with titles like 'Banana in your fruit basket', 'My Stove Is in Good Condition', 'Let Me Play with Your Yo-Yo', and Please warm my Weiner'.

Night after night I slipped out of the tent to find the sources of the music. Follow the pipers. Duos or trios. All you needed was a washboard and a guitar, belting out the old folk tunes, popularised by the skiffle stars. I was the moth and they were the light. But I kept getting caught. Our chiefs regularly counted the boys in the tents. After running out of warnings I was locked in a section of the Scouts village for badly behaved boys. It was a one-day punishment, just on the one day that a young queen Elizabeth, came visiting the camp. While the thousands of Scouts saw her from far away, she cruised past our compound in a fancy black car and waved at us. But there was low-hanging fruit across the fence in the neighbours' yard and no one was going to stop me plucking it. After the Jamboree I was kicked out of the Woudlopers.

The new style had captivated an entire generation of youth in England and beyond. Also Belgium had its own bearded and long-haired king of skiffle, Ferre Grignard. The rough and ready style encouraged amateurs. You did not need expensive instruments or much musical training. If Lonnie could play such exciting music with three chords, a guitar, a washboard and a bass made from a crate, so could anyone. I have read somewhere that some fifty thousand skiffle groups surfaced in Britain alone in the late 1950s, playing at parties, in churches, in coffee bars and cafes. Not only the boy scouts were listening. Donegan's 'Putting on the Style' was number one on the same day Paul McCartney and John Lennon met for the first time, at a gig by Lennon's skiffle band, The Quarrymen, in July 1957, a week before I arrived in Birmingham in a scout uniform. The disc would be the last English chart topper to be solely pressed in 78 rpm format. The times were changing.

It was bands like the Beatles that would hasten the demise of skiffle. 1957 was the illustrious year Elvis recorded 'Heartbreak Hotel'. Some of the boy scout skiffle groups already sang 'That's Alright Mama', 'Rip It Up", Long Tall Sally', ''Shake Rattle and Roll' and 'Blue Suede Shoes'. Lonnie still had some hits to sing, broadening his repertoire with novelty songs in English Music Hall style, as usual, on skiffle steroids. 'Does your Chewing Gum Lose its Flavour' and 'My Old Man's a Dustman'. The Dustman became a popular football chant for the Arsenal football club. But, by the end of the fifties the craze was largely over.

I returned home from the Jamboree 'All Shook Up', and began straining at my leash, starting to peek across the borders. Belgium is so tiny. It is easy to leave. Once I dozed off on a train and woke up in Germany. Two years later I travelled to Manchester to see Lonnie Donegan. The Boy Scouts had opened my door to nature. The Jamboree opened my door to the wider world. Lonnie Donegan opened his door for the Beatles, the Stones and an avalanche of British bands to come through. He is the only star I have ever asked for a signature.

4

LES CHANSONNIERS

The chansonniers, the francophone singer songwriters, were an essential part of our musical culture and, even though American Jazz was very much appreciated, only from the end of the fifties onwards the Anglo-Saxon invaders would encroach on the Belgian airwaves with the explosion of rock. The war songs echoed through my childhood. 'J'attendrai' from France, 'Lili Marleen' from Germany, 'We'll meet again' from Britain. Loaded songs that lasted. When 'La Vie en Rose' was released in 1946 my grandfather hummed the tune behind the counter of his grocery store, my dad suddenly became romantic and, not even me and my brother Eric, still in nappies, could escape the song; it played on high rotation on every radio station.

Édith Piaf, the singer of 'La Vie en Rose', was the queen of the torch ballad. She had written the lyrics to the song. Love and loss were her score. Her image was exemplified in the song 'Milord', written by the French-Egyptian songwriter George Moustaki. Édith represented the girl who was nothing but a 'shadow on the street', most likely a young prostitute who would never catch the interest of the rich Milord. The image was close to the bone. She grew up in a brothel, which her grandmother on her father's side ran in Normandy. Her grandfather was a Moroccan acrobat, her father a street performer and her mother a café singer and circus artiste.

Édith was on the street at a young age, performing in nightclubs and brothels. They nicknamed her La Môme, the Little Sparrow. She was tiny, pretty, but with a ravaged look of someone who knew what suffering meant. Europe, and soon the rest of the world, fell in love with her. 'Non, je ne regrette rien', a song that could rip your heart with a saw, and her hit, 'Padam Padam', were all over the continent. The tragic downward slide of her life played out in full view of us all. The car accidents. The alcohol addiction. Her struggles. She had become a legend before her death at forty-seven in 1963, one of the most celebrated artists of the twentieth century.

Just as important an icon of French culture was Juliette Gréco and the beginning of her life was just as traumatic. Her family had joined the resistance during World War Two. Her mother and sister were deported to a Nazi concentration camp, her sisters were tortured by the Gestapo and Juliette was jailed when she was sixteen. When released, she walked back to Paris and, only much later, she found out her family had been liberated by the Russians.

Juliette had boundless charisma, a voice like velvet, the eyes of a femme fatale, accentuated by her contained stage presence, long black hair over a black dress. She hung out with philosophers and intellectuals. 'Gréco has a million poems in her voice,' wrote Jean-Paul Sartre, who became her friend in the Bohemian circles in the cellars on the Left

Bank of Paris. Her songs were political statements and the finest songwriters and poets wrote for her. Admired by Jean Cocteau and Albert Camus she was nicknamed 'the muse of existentialism'. Radical chic. An activist and a free spirit, she embodied female power and mystique. Gréco was the lover and friend of Miles Davis until his death. When Miles was asked why they did not marry, he replied 'I love her too much to marry her.' She died at ninety-three after seven decades on stage. Francoise Hardy's teenage melancholy and the sensual yearning of Carla Bruni would follow in her footsteps.

Memories of the war still haunted our populations, long after the killing was done. Bomb craters in the town of Mechelen were slowly being filled and rebuilt. As kids we played hide and seek in the bunkers in the fields. The horrors of the war were avoided in conversations, but not forgotten. The most famous anti-war song of the time was 'Le Déserteur', written by Boris Vian and first performed in 1954 by Marcel Mouloudje on the day of the French defeat in the first Indochina war. Boris Vian was a novelist, a poet, a singer and a fine trumpeter in the French jazz scene. He had inherited a distrust of the church and the military from his father, and like Piaf and Gréco, he loved the bohemian life. 'Le Déserteur' was addressed in the form of a letter to the French president from a man explaining his reasons for refusing the call to arms and becoming a deserter.

'I just received
My military papers
To go to war

> Before Wednesday evening
> Mister President
> I don't want to do it
> I'm not on earth
> To kill poor people
> It's not to upset you
> I have to tell you
> I've made my decision
> I'm going to desert
>
> On the roads of France
> From Brittany to Provence
> I will tell people
> refuse to obey
> refuse to do it
> don't go to war
> refuse to leave
> If you have to give blood
> Go give yours
> You are a good apostle
> Mister president'

(excerpt translated from the song 'The Deserter' of Boris Vian)

The song was adopted in many languages, recorded by Peter, Paul and Mary and many others. Joan Baez sang it at anti-Vietnam war demonstrations. It was banned from French radio and TV until 1967, yet it stands as one of the great anti-war songs, together with Bob Dylan's 'Masters of War'. And still history keeps repeating itself. In 1957, the year I attended the Boy Scouts Jamboree in Birmingham, the Campaign for Nuclear Disarmament (CND) was created in the United Kingdom, with Bertrand Russell as its president. It advocated the end of nuclear weapons and opposed the use of chemical and biological weapons. It was a powerful peace movement that spread across Europe in the early 1960s and grew into an anti-war movement, opposing US military bases in Europe and later, the wars in Vietnam and Iraq. It spoke to me and to countless young people, alarmed at the growth of the arms industry after two world wars.

Since then the USA has become addicted and dependent upon its weapons sales, the only country constantly at war. It enwraps the world in a spider's web of military bases and sells more weapons than Russia, China, France and England combined. Frank Zappa only stated a fact when he said: 'Government is the entertainment division of the military-industrial complex.' Donald Trump proudly displayed his weapons sales to Saudi Arabia on TV, while Joe Biden tries to obfuscate his sales to dictators and unsavoury regimes, but every US government, Democrat or Republican, has profited from the suffering and destruction of other countries and populations. The bombs dropped on Vietnam, North Korea, Cambodia, Syria and Iraq, on schools and hospitals in Yemen, on apartment blocks in Gaza, the bombs that maim peasants working the fields of Laos and Afghanistan come with the best wishes of the American government. All its presidents are guilty. Between this gallery of weapons merchants and assassins only Jimmy Carter, a man of moral principle and decency, stands out.

'America is sick and her sickness endangers the whole world', said Bertrand Russell. The national motto 'In God We Trust' should read 'In Guns We Trust' and the 'Stars and Stripes' banner should be replaced by the more realistic 'Bombs and Stripes'. It has become the nation's undoing. 'A Murder Most Foul' Bob Dylan framed it, in perhaps his finest song-poem. The master and the slave. The puritan and the gunslinger. Custer's last stand and the atom bomb on Hiroshima. Beware Disunited States! Beware son. 'Don't take your guns to town.' Who will stage the finale? A Hollywood production streamed in real time? *Gunfight at the O.K. Corral? Apocalypse Now? Dr Strangelove?* I feel the credits coming on. A visit is unlikely. I must bid my adieu by text. Thanks for the fabulous music that has inspired us all. It was your greatest gift. And it will remain, forever floating in our polluted oceans, a magnificent Treasure island, an island of Sirens.

George Brassens too was marked by the war. The Nazis had forced him to work in a labour camp. When he was given ten days leave he went into hiding. A poet, master songwriter and guitarist his warm voice was woven all through my childhood. From small theatres and cafes, on records and on TV, his songs of wit, humor and tenderness radiated throughout the francophone world. His wry sarcasm took aim at the hypocrisy of the bourgeoisie and the church and resonated with everyone. The man with the moustache was the uncle I always wanted to have. From 'Les Amoureux des Bancs Publics' (1953) to 'Les Copains d'abord' (1964) he had me in his thrall, a man with an anarchistic streak and disdain for authority you had to listen to. He wrote two hundred and fifty songs and, he too became an icon of French culture, forever placed in the soundtrack of my life.

But the singer and songwriter that affected me more than anyone came from my home country. Born in Schaerbeek near Brussels from Flemish parents that spoke French at home, Jacques Brel was quintessentially Belgian, recording both in French and Flemish. He accompanied my teenage years into adulthood. His commercial breakthrough came in September 1956 with his recording of 'Quand on n'a que l'amour'. By the end of the decade, he had gained an impressive and enthusiastic following across France. In the early sixties Brel exploded. Like George Brassens, Brel took aim at the bigotry of bourgeois society and the clergy.

I entered Leuven university in 1961 to study law and his songs were on every juke box in the student town. I fell in love with a girl named Nessie, who was a barmaid in a student café run by her religiously conservative Dutch parents. We both loved and identified with Brel. His album *Les Bourgeois* was released in 1962, filled with future classics. 'Madeleine', 'Les Biches' (The Does), 'La Statue' (The Statue), 'La Colombe', another anti-war song, 'Les Bourgeois' and 'Le Plat Pays' (in the Flemish version, 'Mijn Vlakke Land'), a sweeping ode to the low lands of Flanders that will star forever among my favourite songs, a song more poetic and deep than any of what passes for national anthems steeped in jingoism and platitudes, though I must make exceptions for the South African 'Nkosi Sikeleli Afrika', the revolutionary 'La Marseillaise' and the stately 'God Save the Queen'.

I loved Nessie, but ours was like a secret love affair of whispers and smiles across the bar, and although I was not her only suitor, I knew my love was reciprocated. But I had another girlfriend, Beatrice, in my home town of Mechelen, just around the corner. I only managed to take Nessie out on a date once and had to borrow my dad's car to go and pick her up in the countryside of Brabant and return her at 10 pm to her parents' home. Nessie's life was strictly controlled. Meeting her, outside of the bar of her folks, was problematic. She was too unattainable, out of reach, while sex with Beatrice was readily available a few steps away. I let my hormones decide for me, married the wrong girl and Beatrice and I set out to Africa after completing my studies. Nessie phoned me in tears on the day before I left the country.

I only saw her once more, forty years later, at a performance in a bookshop in my home town of Mechelen to launch my first book *Tarab, Travels with my Guitar*. She gave me an email address but it never worked. Perhaps she thought it wiser for us not to meet again. But my love for Jacques Brel will always connect me with her.

Stupendous songs kept coming: 'Marieke', 'Les Flamandes' (Flemish Women), 'Le Moribond' (The Dying Man), 'Amsterdam', 'La Valse à Mille Temps' (The Thousand-Beat Waltz), 'Mathilde', 'Vesoul', 'Je Suis un Soir d'été' (I am a Summer's Evening), 'La Chanson des Vieux Amants' (The Song of Old Lovers), which I recorded on my album *The House is Empty*. Poetry in motion. His songs were literate, his performances theatrical with the emotional and physical energy of a cyclone that would put his audience in a frenzy and could teach Mick Jagger a thing or two. He starred in ten movies and acted the part of Don Quixote in *L'Homme de la Mancha*, a musical he composed adapting Cervantes' famous work. He was Belgium's best-selling recording artist of all time with over twenty-five million records sold. His songs were recorded by Ray Charles, Nina Simone, Frank Sinatra, Shirley Bassey, David Bowie and John Denver. Jacques Brel gave me a code to live by:

> 'Le rire est dans le coeur
> Le mot dans le regard
> Le coeur est voyaguer
> L'avenir est au hazard
> ('Les Marquises')
> Laughter is in the heart
> The word is in the gaze
> The heart is a traveller
> The future is open to chance

Brel was a poet who burned like a torch and gave us his all in every performance of his gruelling touring schedule. He had been a chain smoker his whole life and it would be his undoing. He decided to retire in 1966 with a series of farewell concerts, including at Carnegie Hall, where the American press called him 'an electric storm'. In 1974 he left Europe on his yacht to sail around the world but was soon diagnosed with advanced lung cancer. He settled in the Marquesas islands of French Polynesia. He died at forty-nine and was buried there, his grave a few metres away from the tomb of Paul Gauguin, the painter. Jacques Brel left us a towering body of work and was one of the most important songwriters of the twentieth century.

'Mijn vlakke land'—'Le Plat Pays'—My Flat Country

When the rain falls on streets, squares and flower beds
On the roof and spire of sky-high churches
Which are the only mountains in this flat land
When under the clouds people are dwarfs
When the days go in stupid regularity
And a bulging east wind beats the land even flatter
Then my land awaits
My flat country

When the low sky skims right over the water
When the low sky teaches us humility
When the low sky is gray as slate
When the low sky is pale as boulder clay
When the north wind quarters the plain
When the north wind steals our breath away
Then my land cracks
My flat country

When the Scheldt shimmers in the southern sun
And every Flemish woman strolls in a summer-dress
When the first spider weaves its spring web
Or steaming fields in July sunlight tremble
When the south wind roars through the grain
When the south wind exults along the track
Then my country rejoices
My flat country

(excerpt freely translated from the Flemish version by Jacques Brel and Ernst van Altena)

LES CHANSONNIERS

Many chansonniers would follow in the footsteps of these giants of song. Perhaps the most famous, and notorious, was the son of Jewish Ukrainian migrants who had fled after the Russian revolution, Serge Gainsbourg. The family had to flee a second time when the Nazis invaded France. The yellow star to identify him as a Jew haunted Serge for the rest of his life. Serge was a bad boy, provocative and scandalous. His biography is filmed by one of my favourite graphic artists Joann Sfar, another exiled Jew, with an intellect so French and sophisticated it would bypass most Anglo-Saxon readers, and only a fraction of his work has been translated in English, the most famous the series *A Rabbi's Cat* about a house cat that talks critical philosophy with a rabbi.

Gainsbourg came to my attention in 1963 with 'La Javanaise' which he wrote for Juliette Greco, and then with his monster hit, 'Je t'aime... moi non plus', written for Brigitte Bardot, but recorded with Jane Birkin in 1969, after the protests of Bardot's husband. Many countries banned it and the simulated sex and heavy breathing enraged the Vatican. But on my return from Africa I found the Catholic church in terminal decline in Belgium. Monasteries were closing, churches emptied, priests got married, the black frocks were out of fashion. Soon I left Europe again to travel east and Gainsbourg, as well as most French culture, disappeared from my radar for many years. As my life moved on so did the soundtracks. Only decades on I would discover the breadth of Gainsbourg's work that made him a legend.

5

LONNIE JOHNSON

What was I doing, hailing a cab in the pouring rain at three in the morning in New York city with my young son asleep on my shoulder? A canary taxi swerved to the curb and the driver swung the door wide open.

'Paul! Is that you?'

I was flabbergasted. I had not seen my cousin Paul in years but since I began keeping a dream diary I have discovered that I have allies in my dreams who advise me, sometimes saving me from a precarious situation such as grabbing my shoulder when I am about to fall from a precipice. So, even though I had not seen my cousin since childhood, he regularly appears as a dream ally.

Paul smiled and I slid inside, my boy on my lap. We drove off with the windscreen wipers straining, rain slashing. My boy was awake.

'Look daddy.' He pointed at the elegant chrome lettering on the dashboard. It read: *Lonnie Johnson*.

'Lonnie Johnson! Is that the name of this car?'

'It is,' said Paul.

'I have never heard of such a model. But one of my

favourite guitarists and blues singers is called Lonnie Johnson.'

'That's him.'

'The one with the sweetest voice, crooner of the blues?'

'Sure is. And I know a club where we can hear him play at this hour of the night in New York city,' said Paul with a grin and took a sharp turn to the right.

'Wet night, sir.'

The doorman of the club did not notice that I hid my boy beneath my raincoat.

Inside it was dry, smoky and dim. I took a seat and ordered a Bourbon whiskey. There was a murmur and hands clapping in the dark. Then Lonnie Johnson stepped into my dream. White shirt beneath a satin suit, shimmering in the lights, a diamond guitar stickpin on his tie. He always was an impeccable dresser, looking like the maître d'hôtel, the major domo of the blues. He bowed, unleashed a flurry of single note magic from his guitar and turned inward, self-contained, his child-like face absorbed in the music. Not a glance at the audience, the smile guarded till his departure from the stage. His slender body hardly moved, except for his fingers dancing up and down the fretboard. Yet the lack of showmanship was eclipsed by his class and effortless virtuosity. And then he sang with the sweetest and most aching voice I had ever heard:

> 'Well it's too late to cry, baby
> Your last chance is gone
> It's too late to cry, baby
> Your best man is gone'

It cut through the bone and made you feel like weeping. My son was asleep on my lap while I was wide-eyed, shivering when he broke into his one big hit 'Tomorrow Night', a song later covered by a young Elvis Presley, recorded in the Memphis Sun studio in 1954. Elvis mimicked Lonnie's crooning style and it can be heard in many of the king's ballads and blues throughout his career. The song had also been a standard in my own repertoire, though I never came close to emulating Lonnie's masterful singing: the extended notes, the jazz phrasing, the yearning, the honeyed tonsils. I wish!

The first record I bought from my Uncle Fernand's shop was a Big Bill Broonzy LP. I didn't buy it for myself since I didn't have the money saved up yet to purchase a record player. I bought it for my school friend, Alfons', thirteenth birthday. He was not amused. Big Bill didn't do it for him.

'If you don't live it you don't have it,' said Big Bill Broonzy.

I hadn't lived it, but this boy had fallen in love with the blues. It spoke to me. Brownie McGhee, John Lee Hooker and Jimmy Reed torched my bedroom curtains and showed me the neon halos round the moon, when I should have been doing my homework. In hindsight I can appreciate my rigid upbringing. It taught me self-discipline, concentration and persistence. But as a youngster I felt boxed in, corralled by family, church and middle class society, the rigid timetables and studies. There was no other side of the tracks in Mechelen, a traditional town in Flanders. World War II had left Europe battle-scarred and exhausted—sedated by new toasters and Electrolux vacuum cleaners. After seeing Disney's *Peter Pan* film I prayed by my open window for Peter to come and whisk me away to his island. Peter did not come, setting me on the road to atheism. But take it from me: if you really, really want it, you will find that every room hides a magic step-in wardrobe or an enchanted mirror.

Mine stood around the corner from my parents' house: the municipal library of my home town, to which I owe eternal gratitude. This noble institution possessed, beside books, a vast collection of jazz, classical and rare folk records from around the world. Not even the great Library of Alexandria had these. I only needed to walk two hundred metres to borrow half a dozen records that transported me somewhere else. The librarian held the LP under a light and each scratch was dutifully notated on a small card slipped into a pocket attached to the record sleeve; if you were a regular scratcher you lost your right as a borrower. And so I discovered John Coltrane and Cannonball Adderley, Brazilian guitarists Laurindo Almeida and Baden Powell, the hereditary griots from Mali, the drummers from Burundi and the ragas from India.

Mechelen's municipal library was also a treasure grove of American folk, blues and gospel –then called Negro spirituals. The beating heart of old America: Leadbelly, Blind Lemon Jefferson, Cisco Houston, Muddy Waters, Woody Guthrie, Sonny Terry and Brownie McGhee, Sister Rosetta Tharpe, the Golden Gate quartet, the Harry Smith quintessential anthology of American folk music: boxcar songs, brothel songs, work songs, drinking and party songs, murder songs, hollers and holy songs that revealed the real world out there, hidden from view in a post-war sanitised small town. These were the songs I sang in my bedroom and on my first excursions around Western Europe. My first EP recorded in 1965 during a road trip through Germany with Irish folk singer Geoff Iliff featured a blues for a girl named 'Rosaline'. But there were no Lonnie Johnson records in the library and it was only in the early 1960s when he toured Europe with the American Folk Blues Festival, among many giants of the blues, that Lonnie appeared on my radar. The legendary harp player Sonny Boy Williamson introduced him and the ace band of Otis Spann, Willie Dixon, and Bill Stepney accompanied him on piano, bass and drums. How come I had not heard of this guy? I was in for a surprise.

Alonzo Johnson was born in New Orleans in 1894. Everyone called him Lonnie and the nickname stuck. At the turn of the century New Orleans was a melting pot of races and musical genres, the incubator of blues and jazz. Music was all around. Both of his parents played instruments and so did most of his ten siblings. His dad taught him the violin and guitar and soon the boy joined his father's band at parties and weddings, going out busking for coins on street corners. But tragedy struck in 1918 when Johnson's father and nine other members of his family died, victim to the flu epidemic. Thus commenced the dramatic rollercoaster ride that was Lonnie's destiny.

The memories were too much to bear and he and his remaining brother James left New Orleans for Saint Louis, finding gigs around town and playing the violin on the Mississippi riverboats. Though Lonnie excelled in many styles he entered a blues singing contest and won. It led to a recording contract and Johnson's career took off. Between 1925 and 1932 he made 130 recordings and had his first hits. The guitar now replaced the violin as his main instrument. He toured with Bessie Smith, recorded with Louis Armstrong and Duke Ellington and had his own radio show in New York. Lonnie had become a star and a role model for African-Americans, downtrodden by vicious oppression and racism. A well-mannered, dignified, sophisticated, elegant urban black man in a fine suit, a virtuoso musician who could play blues or jazz, a soulful singer and songwriter in tune with the woes and heartaches of the people around him was an inspiration to all.

In 1929 he recorded ten instrumental masterpieces with the white guitarist Eddie Lang that entered the annals of guitar history. It was sheer brilliance. One could argue that Johnson was the man who brought the guitar from its role as a rhythm provider to the foreground as a solo instrument, paving the way for what was to come. His duets with Eddie Lang were among the first to feature black and white musicians performing together. Then the Great Depression changed everything. The music industry went in decline. Bookings dried up and Lonnie's luck ran out. He went back to the steel mill in East St. Louis. 'I started as a sander, and ended up as a moulder. Moulding big box car wheels, that's what I was moulding', he said in an interview.

By the end of the thirties we find him back on the playing circuit, this time in Chicago, the boom town that attracted thousands of Negroes coming up from the south to escape rural poverty and find employment in the steel works. The Great Migration. Clubs and bars mushroomed, the blues went electric and so did Johnson. Back in the studio he recorded first blues, then ballads. Johnson was an emotional and romantic man, prone to burst into tears when recording his heartbreak songs and in 1948 he scored his first pop hit with 'Tomorrow Night', a song he did not write but had taken a liking to. It sold three million copies. He bought a large house, toured England, though his recent sweet ballads did not always go down well with an audience that wanted raw blues. By the time he returned home he found himself out of demand and returned to the steel foundry and other jobs. He had money problems, could not meet paying the mortgage on his house and disappeared into obscurity. He never handled his finances well, a ladies man who spent a lot on women. Johnson was history. But he always knew his worth.

'I have been dead four or five times, but I always come back. Someday, somebody would find me.'

Indeed people thought he was dead. Till, in 1959, Chris Albertson, a jazz radio DJ in Philadelphia, played a Lonnie Johnson track and, when wondering on air whatever happened to the artist, received a call from somebody at a hotel in town who said, 'I work with somebody named Lonnie Johnson. He's a janitor, he never talks about music. But he's very careful with his hands. He always uses gloves.'

The DJ got Lonnie on his show, brought him back in the studio and helped engineer his third comeback. It was the right time. The folk and blues revival had lit up the USA music scene. Young musicians rediscovered Harry Smith's anthology of American folk music. Suddenly the old bluesmen and rural traditionalists were cool again and many a legend emerged from the dark, including Lonnie Johnson. He quit his job as a janitor at the hotel and started touring. In 1963 he joined the American Folk Blues Festival in the company of Big Joe Williams, Willie Dixon, Memphis Slim and others for the series of electrifying concerts that brought him to my attention. I was not the only one. The Rolling Stones, Eric Clapton, Eric Burdon and Stevie Winwood all saw some of these riveting shows and we all know where that led. The English boys brought it all back to the USA, where these legendary men had been forgotten.

But gigs in the USA soon dried up once more as the interest in folk evaporated. Bob Dylan had gone electric, psychedelic rock was the fashion. But Lonnie was not done yet. The Metro Stompers, a Canadian Dixieland jazz band based in Toronto, invited him to play some shows with them. The audiences adored him. He was 71 and decided to base himself in Toronto. His five years in the city were his final act. In March 1969 disaster struck again. Lonnie was standing on the sidewalk outside a restaurant when two cars smashed into each other. One flew on to the pavement and hit Lonnie. He fell forward and then the second car hit him. He was seriously injured, suffering a broken hip and kidney injuries. A benefit concert was held but Lonnie never fully recovered from his injuries and suffered a stroke in February of the next year, He was 76.

And still, many music lovers have not heard of Johnson and his music. He was a versatile musician and crossed over from blues into jazz and romantic ballads. Perhaps this smooth urban singer, guitar wizard and songwriter did not fit the mould and the expectations of white listeners who only saw the prototype of raw and rural Delta blues singers like John Lee Hooker, Son House and Lightning Hopkins, men who had suffered many an injustice in the southern cotton fields and who often recycled phrases from the previous standard blues repertoire. Yet Lonnie influenced generations of musicians that followed, from Django Reinhardt and B. B. King to Chuck Berry and Eric Clapton. Buddy Holly and Bob Dylan were fans. The British king of skiffle swapped his name from Tony to Lonnie Donegan in his honour. The Rolling Stones' former bass player, Bill Wyman, called him 'the original guitar hero'. Lonnie Johnson was a trailblazer, a gentle, dignified man who never bragged, a man you would invite into your home.

6
ROCK&ROLL

lgebra class. Thirty boys locked in a room with a priest in a black frock and a blackboard with formulas. Thirty wooden desks that previous generations of boys had carved and inked their scribblings on. Historical maps of boredom. I gazed out of the widow at the sparrows fluttering and frolicking in the thick of the tree branches above the deserted playground. A melodious ether infused the warm afternoon sky. From the top of the Saint Rombouts cathedral the carillon beamed its tinkling carols and canticles all over the town of Mechelen, a lure beckoning from an out-of-reach wonderland. The monotone murmur of constants and variables, exponents and equations put me in a slumber, a lost soul in an alien world, trapped in a regimented existence. I spent my days like a hamster on a wheel. I learned and memorised countless facts and dates, numbers and languages, rules and regulations, meaningless exercises in rote learning, while being spoon-fed sacrosanct dogmas and pious examples.

I had not formed an identity yet, a foot soldier with sergeants all around. I did not have a flag to raise. I was just dodging bullets. Everything seemed predetermined. That is, until I built a small transistor radio inside one of my grandfather's cigar boxes and Radio Luxemburg popped up. When I plugged in, the grey fields of my youth blossomed. Flowers burst into fireworks. The broadcaster was the prototype pirate station, playing music each night no other station did. The new music came out of the USA, via Luxemburg: rhythm and blues, rock and roll, country and western, the latest hits. Its powerful transmitter reached far and wide, switching on a generation of European post-war teenagers. Ducklings broke out of their eggshells. Madmen ripped off their strait jackets. When 'Johnny be Good' crackled from my cigar box, all at once the world turned, on the beat and off my seat, from black and white to colour. 'Be-Bop-a-Lula', 'Great Balls of Fire', 'Shakin' all over', 'Roll over Beethoven'. Outrageous songs, daredevil singers that challenged my presumptions and unleashed my angst. Songs like mantras, talismans and gris-gris, spells to exorcise my Catholic high school demons, to nix the tantum ergos of chapel disciplinarians in frocks, lift their hocus pocus masks and free the saints to boogie on their fine-grained marble pedestals. I could not resist and let the gods and demons possess me. Thus, when 'Lucille', 'Maybelline' and 'Peggy Sue' came calling, my brain went on vacation and I had to repeat a whole year at school. My parents nor teachers could figure out what had happened. My uncle Louis chased me down the street when he came home to 'Tutti Frutti', blasting from his 'classical only' record cabinet, my cousin and I jumping about like wind-up toys, yelling 'Wop-bop-a-loo-bop-a-boom-bam-boom'. Later I learned that the song was about anal sex, but I never told my uncle.

ROCK&ROLL

Every year a fair would be mounted in the main square and the whole town would turn out to ride the Caterpillar, the Pendulum and the Roller Coaster, canter on the Carousel of Bejewelled Horses. Everyone shrieked in the Haunted Castle, guffawed and jeered in the House of Mirrors. On the fairground a shooting and a throw-a-prize gallery stood side by side under a canvas roof. A little girl with a tulle blue dress won a giant panda bear, throwing the darts. Pink candy sticks and ice cream parlours. Mouth-watering beignets—deep-fried doughnuts filled with custard, coated with icing sugar. And now, a large amusement ride of bumper cars -or dodgems if you are more of a dodger than a bumper- had been set up right next to the post office and it blasted all the latest juke box hits by Gene Vincent, Bill Haley, Carl Perkins, Elvis, Chuck, Fats, Buddy, Richard, Jerry Lee and the Everly Brothers. The guys working the bumper cars wore jeans and black leather jackets, greased hair and duck tails, chewed gum and blew smoke, fancied themselves Elvis or Gene, skating across the tin floor, hanging off the collector pole at the back of the cars, swinging from car to car like gibbons from the trees, while the kids bumped and dodged. The town dignitaries disapproved but a generational divide had crept into the system. A spanner in the wheels of the 1950s. Lots of little rebels on the loose without a cause.

Wurlitzer jukeboxes and pinball machines appeared in milk bars, cafes and pubs. Suddenly music was everywhere. I swapped my banjo-mandolin for a guitar and formed a rock band. Our drummer was still learning to keep the beat, bass players came and went, but Hendrik, our lead guitarist and a hairdresser, could play 'Apache' by the Shadows, just like the record, including the echo effect. I learned to play the piano intro to 'What did I Say' and sang Buddy Holly, Little Richard and Johnny Kid and the Pirates at dances and parties. My best friend, Bo, took photographs of me standing in front of my bedroom curtain, holding a cheap microphone, pretending to sing. We called ourselves The Dragons and I became Chris Kent, after the cigarettes I smoked as a youngster. My dad, my brother and I, we all smoked, pacing around the house, ash trays in every room. Even my mother would occasionally relax with a cigarette after the evening meal was done. It was a fantasy of the fifties. My parents disapproved of my musical antics, fearful of the family reputation being soiled. They had something else in mind, a different vision of my future. *Father knows Best* was the popular TV series of the time and my parents loved it. It featured a successful insurance salesman and model husband with an adoring wife at home with three kids and new household gadgets. Another fantasy of the fifties.

When I first heard Little Richard and Jerry Lee Lewis I lost all reason and went hysterical. Richard and Jerry Lee were sorcerers from somewhere Down South. 'Long Tall Sally' and 'A Whole lot of Shaking Going on' caused steel walls to melt and rusted fences to snap. The heavy velvet curtains that screened me from reality burst into flames. A bolt of lightning shot through me. Cycling to school on the wet cobble stones the following morning my gears had switched from dull to dangerous. It made you walk faster, awoke the third eye.

While Fats Domino arrived in an old taxi like your favourite uncle, a genial smile and a voice stewed in gumbo, Little Richard flew in on the airship Hindenburg and exploded in a ball of fire of hydrogen and helium, screaming and hollering and whooping, part preacher part satyr. With hair like a wedding tart, a pencil moustache and facial pancake he squealed and screeched, his leg on the piano, a hand grenade about to blow up. 'Ooh! My Soul'. His all black band in white suits, The Upsetters, swayed their glittering saxophones from side to side, stepping the quarter hour clockwise with every first beat of the bar. Little Richard bewitched and hexed you. He had worked in the fast disappearing traveling medicine shows that for a century had crisscrossed the rural American towns, mixing music and burlesque with commerce, using songs and performers as the soap box to sell snake oil—and in previous times, had featured white musicians in blackface, lampooning stereotyped African singers and dancers. Richard used to perform in drag as Princess Lavonne, and now girls threw their panties at him. Girls black and white. He wore capes and suits studded with gems and sequins. Suitcases full of dollar bills and Dionysian orgies. Exciting, wild and unpredictable. Until one night in 1957 at a concert in Sydney he saw a red fireball flying across the sky above him and took it as a sign of God telling him to stop playing his devilish music. He threw his four diamond rings in the Hunter river, renounced rock and roll and became a preacher. What he had seen was the launching of the first Russian satellite, the Sputnik.

Jerry Lee Lewis, a lewd mythical demon from Alabama, was the offspring of Atilla the Hun or Genghis Khan, take your pick. A dangerous man. He lay siege to the rich kingdom of Troy, high upon a hill, charged its walls of stone and gates of oak, his pumping piano his Trojan Horse, as, howling and roaring, he burst into the palace, burned down the temples of propriety, pillaged the silos of grain, smashed the amphoras of wine, and like Adonis, combed his waving, blond curls before taking the village virgins for his pleasure. 'Great Balls of Fire!' He was a meteorite of molten talent, and I adored Jerry. A diamond in the rough. Every song he sang, he made his own. After the media sharks in the United Kingdom learned that he had married his thirteen-year-old cousin, his tour was cancelled, the outrage sanctimonious and all his singles were for sale for half a dollar in the cheap bins at every department store in Mechelen. Jerry Lee too, soon disappeared from view.

Everything seemed possible now. A perfumed pompadour, hair dyed scarlet red, do the splits, walk like a duck, stand on the piano, or set it on fire while the punters smashed the chairs. In comparison Buddy Holly looked rather ordinary. A rock singer in a suit who wore a pair of thick, black horn-rimmed glasses and wrote his own songs? His ordinariness gave me licence to dream. I idolised him. When on a Saturday night my cousin Paul and I listened to 'Words of Love' over and over, slumped over the table with a cigarette, Buddy spoke to us personally. It was a song of rare intimacy and deep yearning. The spell of the tom tom rumble, the sparkling Telecaster guibourg and Jane Birkin put their lovemaking on to disk with 'Je t'aime... moi non plus', a song Serge had written for Brigitte Bardot. The song gave me déjà vu. It was the x-rated version of 'Words of Love.'

Every hit song that Buddy plucked from the Tree of Plenty made my hair stand up. Songs, less than three minutes long, of utter perfection. 'That 'll be the Day', 'Well All Right', 'Peggy Sue', 'Rave on', 'Not Fade Away' and 'Heartbeat' still tingle my spine all these years later. Buddy Holly was my imaginary friend. I was obsessed with him. My friend Bo always joked that when I grew up, I would lecture and write about Buddy Holly. And here I am fulfilling his prophecy. Buddy's band, the Crickets was the archetypal rock band. Two electric guitars, bass and drums. From The Dragons to The Beatles, everyone copied the model. When his plane crashed in the dead of winter in a snow-covered corn field in Iowa I felt forsaken by the older brother I never had. Buddy was only twenty-two but in just two years he had left an awe-inspiring body of work and one could only speculate what he would have done if he had lived. Holly was Lennon and McCartney in one man. The Beatles named themselves after The Crickets and recorded his songs and so did the Stones. Bob Dylan and Bruce Springsteen performed them live. Paul McCartney bought the publishing rights to Holly's song catalogue. Elton John started wearing horn-ringed glasses and I recorded a version of 'Heartbeat' in three languages as the opening track of side two on an album recorded in Brazil, *Love is a Phantom*.

Along with Buddy Holly, Chuck Berry and Johnny Cash

were the songwriters paving a new tradition. Songs that never grew old, stood the test of time like the pyramids. 'Crying, Waiting Hoping', 'The Promised Land', 'Big River'. You could not avoid Chuck Berry, or the countless bands that have covered or copied his songs, whatever age you were. Does anyone not know that Beethoven has been rolled over? You wouldn't have to search long around Australia's pubs, parties and clubs to hear his opening riffs. A band that can't play any of his songs might not be called a band. And any songwriter should check out his lyrics. Chuck was the poet and the mechanic of rock. He wired the circuitry. When NASA launched the Voyager spacecraft on its way to Jupiter, and beyond, 'Johnny B Goode' was on board, imprinted on a golden disc to give extraterrestials, one day perhaps, the chance to dance and sing along with the Father, the Shakespeare, the Big Wazoo of rock and roll, America's greatest export: Chuck Berry.

Over time I have been revaluating the lives of these rock and roll showmen, brimming with talent and panache, and their often flawed characters. I have pondered how we struggle to separate the art from the artist. And we should. The artist fades. The art can keep thrilling and inspiring us. Trust the tale, not the teller, the song not the singer. Life is a river, not a canal. It winds. It floods over its banks. And Chuck's life had its turbulence. The law was often after him in a time when any black man was a target. Berry was released from the reformatory on his 21st birthday in 1947 after having been convicted of armed robbery while still in high school. He took a job in a car assembly plant, began playing with the Johnnie Johnson trio that created the fusion of country and rhythm and blues that made him a legend. His first record, 'Maybellene', sold over a million copies. The hits and magic kept coming. He had his own night club in Saint Louis, a guitar-shaped swimming pool, he featured in movies. Then, in the early sixties, at the peak of his fame, he was arrested again, this time for transporting a fourteen-year-old girl across state lines to work in his club. Sure, they probably had sex, but then whenever this brown-eyed handsome man rolled his eyes from the stage, and sang

> 'Close up your books, get out of your seat
> Down the halls and into the street
> Up to the corner and 'round the bend
> Right to the juke joint, you go in' ('Schooldays')

his audience of such young girls were wetting their panties. Berry served one and one-half years in prison, from February 1962 to October 1963. There were accusations of abuse against women, poor behaviour and disdain for his audience. And why would any musician hire any old pick up-band without a rehearsal? No set list. No keys. Just 'One two three! Follow me! Stop when I raise my leg.' Where was his musical pride? Berry did not even bother to speak to the band after the show, evaporated into the night with his guitar and his cash. Yet, in the end, my gripes vanish whenever I put the needle on the disc and all is readily forgotten. Chuck Berry has departed but his music is still travelling on somewhere past Saturn, according to the latest reports.

Johnny Cash was not a man you messed around with. Look at him! A mug shot of a robber, a daguerreotype of an Indian chief. Something about him of the fairground boxer on a trigger, an Old Testament horse whisperer. He was intense and authentic, and you had to respect him, take him for his word. Born in Arkansas in 1932, he worked the fields as a boy with his family and they all sang while picking cotton. After a stint in the army, stationed in Germany as a code operator to spy on the Russians, he turned up at Sun Records in Memphis in 1955 with his gospel tunes and was cast, in the image of Elvis, as a rockabilly star instead. But Johnny was not a wiggler of hips, did not thrust his pelvis at the girls, kept his sex appeal on a leash. His heat radiated on its own. He was a spiritual man and a brilliant folk singer, not a rock star, a noble spirit like Woody Guthrie or Paul Robeson, who stood up for the down-trodden, championed the plight of American Indians, sang for the toughest men in the toughest prisons. The man in black. Over a thousand songs. Songs written in tablets by the finger of God. 'I Walk the Line' and 'Get Rhythm', has my vote for the Best Single of all times (1955). At least until 1967 when 'Penny Lane' and 'Strawberry Fields Forever' were released.

Bob Dylan once sang 'In the dime stores and bus stations people talk of situations, read books, repeat quotations, draw conclusions on the wall.' ('Love Minus Zero/No Limit') And so it is with all the talk of 'Who was the king of rock and roll?' Elvis or Chuck? The Stones or the Beatles? Van Gogh or Gauguin? Does anyone really care? The first time I saw Presley was in 1957, the year I returned from the Boy Scout Jamboree in Birmingham. I was spending the school holidays with my parents and siblings on the Flemish seaside and hitchhiked to Mechelen to see the movie

Love Me Tender. It was a western set in the years following the Civil War. There were no American Indians and it was more of a Greek tragedy with pistols instead of knives, an archetypal conflict of jealousy between brothers. Elvis—Clint in the film—had married his older brother's fiancée, believing him to have died in the war. Then the brother returned. In the finale climax Elvis was shot, which was somewhat disappointing, but before that he got his chance to sing at a hoedown, demonstrating his fancy legwork and shaking like jelly while the nineteenth century country girls swung their long skirts, yelled and whooped. I had been told that in America the girls screamed in the movie theatres, but they did not in Mechelen. I was only one of four people in the stalls. He crooned the sentimental title track but I was into the fast stuff.

Better films followed: *Loving You, Jailhouse Rock, King Creole*. Then it rolled downhill with an endless wimpy movie career. But I bought all these early albums. 'Mystery Train' was my favourite song. I was always waiting in anticipation for that last wolf howl in the fade-out of the record. A train ride to bliss in two minutes and twenty-seven seconds. When I heard 'One Night' for the first time, I tumbled two storeys down the stairs of our family home in frenzied ecstasy. It hit me like a meteor and I went radio-active. The song was a hormonal ode to lust, a discharge of delivery, a desperate sexual yearning, echoed by Bruce Springsteen, years later, with 'I'm On Fire'.

Presley was a force of nature, but when he left the army he came out sterilised, pasteurised and packaged, a play toy and the golden goose of his manager Colonel Parker, just another teen idol in the mould of Fabian and Frankie Avalon, a mannequin at Walmart, a clone of his former self, only performing in Las Vegas, when not locked up in Graceland to casually morph into a Big Mac hamburger. I lost track of Elvis, Jerry Lee, Little Richard and Johnny Cash. My life moved on but the songs remained. Music of timeless beauty that dismissed the illusion of a world that marches towards progress. By the end of the fifties the bushfire that was rock and roll was contained and blandness returned. But only for a short while.

7

JESSE FULLER

In 1961 I took a ferry from Ostend to Dover and a train to London with my buddy Pol to hunt down rare folk records I could not obtain in my native Belgium. I had been making the crossing during my school holidays to rummage through the plethora of record shops in the city and to rove around Soho in search of live music. My regular hangout was a grungy little cave, down a narrow staircase on Old Compton street, the 2 i's Coffee Bar. Here skiffle bands and early rock acts sharpened their axes in a fog of cigarette smoke and the nebulous glimmer of a couple of low watt light bulbs. The Vipers, Vince Taylor and Johnny Kid let loose on a stage of milk crates and boards, backs against the wall. There was no entry charge. Only a service counter with a coffee machine, orange juice and sandwiches. The cellar was always packed, but it was tiny. It only had room for a couple of dozen punters, besides the band. Cliff Richard and Tommy Steele had started out there, though I never got to see them. The early sixties were a lull between two cyclones, catamarans adrift with limp sails on a flat ocean, skippers asleep. The Beatles were still playing all night long at the Top Ten Club in Hamburg for sailors, drunks and hookers. The fury of rock and roll had abated. The roaring tides of the Mersey Beat, hard rock, psychedelic rock, soul and folk still to come. Roy Orbison's 'Crying' was on the hit parade, as were Patsy Cline's 'I Fall to Pieces' and Del Shannon's 'Runaway'. But it was the folk and blues records on obscure and small labels I was searching for.

And so I bought this album by Jesse Fuller, the original one-man band, a San Francisco busker who accompanied himself on a twelve-string guitar, harmonica, kazoo, cymbals and a self-built contraption he named the fotdella, a suitcase-like six-string bass viol which he played with his foot using a system of levers and pedals.

Born in poverty in Georgia, his mother had left him as a toddler with a family that 'treated me worse than a dog,' leaving him starved and beaten. He never knew his father. Jesse worked in labour camps in the south, iced cars on the Southern Pacific, hobo-ed the freight trains, shined shoes in a barber shop, carved wooden snakes which he sold on the sidewalks for a dollar and married happily. When the folk boom emerged like a butterfly, Jesse got attention and Alan Lomax invited him as a guest of honour at a folk festival on the Berkeley campus in 1959, earning him fifty dollars. A tour of Europe followed. It was his first time on an aeroplane. In Belfast he was carried on the shoulders of enthusiastic fans like a soccer star and his song, 'San Francisco Bay Blues', has since become an American classic. I was leaving college then and would soon start university. The album somehow found its way back to me, like an old dog tracks his master, and, when I took it out of its sleeve and lowered the needle of my record player, these memories flooded my mind.

8
FOLK

They opened the cell at 9 am, gave me a bowl of onion soup, and a policeman pushed me out in the street with a warning. I smelled the summer Parisian air and made for the Halles, the old food market in the heart of the city, guitar in hand, a small bag over my shoulder with my diary, wallet with busking money, passport and some underwear. I wore a pair of jeans, a frilly white blouse given to me by an English girl after my backpack was stolen in Ibiza, and my piece de resistance, a pair of boots of Spanish leather, purchased in Barcelona in honour of the famous Bob Dylan song. Dylan had a hold on me. With every album he released, he had cleared the decks, redrawn the map and, all of a sudden, the tunes of old craftsmen like Johnny Mercer, Cole Porter, Rogers and Hammerstein smacked of bland entertainment. The contemporary songwriters that had stoked the engines of American popular song from their cubicles in the Brill Building in New York—Gerry Goffin and Carole King, Neil Sedaka, Doc Pomus and Mort Shuman—faced an existential crisis. I had been lucky to have my guitar and passport with me. Two policemen had found me sleeping under one of the bridges over the Seine, locked me in a paddy wagon and took me to the station. It was my third encounter with the police in recent weeks. The French gendarmes had been cool, unlike Franco's Guardia Civil who had arrested me in Barcelona for busking and the dour cops who expelled me from the island of Ibiza after I reported the theft of my belongings and, when asked where I was lodging, admitted that I had been sleeping in a cave. Ibiza was not the tourist and party mecca it would become later.

I was still a reluctant law student at Leuven university, hanging in there to please my parents who had invested in me, but my absences grew longer. While most of my fellow students planned careers, my head was spinning with folk, blues and ragas, my brain rewired with the writings of Camus, Steinbeck, Hesse and Marcuse, the beat poets Kerouac and Ginsberg. I felt stuck on the wrong planet, my life steered by others. So, whenever my three month break from university came along I took on odd jobs, painting army barracks, working nightshifts at the Marie-Tumas factory canning peas, tomatoes and beans, or day shifts at the docks of the port of Antwerp, offloading ingots of copper and hefty bunches of pale green bananas from the Congo boats. Each bar of copper needed two men to lift it and a bunch of bananas required one man to haul it, while another tailed him with a stick, in case of the occasional stowaway adder or tarantula that had come along for the trip. For the return journey to Matadi we loaded bags of cement that came sliding down from a ramp on to your shoulders. The first bag flattened me on the ground to the merriment of the experienced dockworkers, but I learned.

With enough money saved up I hitched south, getting a taste of the hobo life the Beats wrote about. I needed to get a grip on my destiny, broaden my vision. Leaving a small country like Belgium was easy. Within a day I would be in Frankfurt, sleeping in a field in Provence, on my way to Italy, Spain or Yugoslavia. Time accelerates when you're on the move. And so does experience. There were marvels to be chanced upon that Mechelen did not offer, more to be learned on the road than in the stale law faculty. 'The world is a book, and those who do not travel read only a page,' said Saint Augustine. That same afternoon, on my way to the Halles, I bumped into my Flemish mate Jannie in a Paris metro station. He acted unsurprised. I was thrilled.

'Jan! What are you doing here?'

'I am on my way to the Congo.'

Jannie was a teenage renegade, younger and taller than me. He wore an army jacket from a disposal store. His blonde hair fell from a blue civil war cap. He made you think that he had returned from fighting the Yankees in the Mexican war in 1846 and was on the run after seducing the corporal's wife in the stable. Jannie was a ladies man, a traveller who would remain a juvenile at heart until he died fifty years later, peacefully in a chair on his lunch break from a carpentry job. We would meet in the oddest places and continents throughout our lives and became compadres. He too suspected that there must be another door somewhere to someplace where life meant something more. He had come fresh from Mechelen. I had come from Spain where I had been playing in a rowdy Catalan bar in Sitges, mainly frequented by Swedish youths relishing a drinking binge, freed from the Swedish alcohol prohibition. I would yell 'Twist and Shout' and 'If had had a Hammer' at the top of my lungs standing on a table while drunks, between or sometimes during songs, attempted to pour red wine or cava from a glass wine pitcher, the porró, into my mouth, drenching my shirt.

Jannie was impressed.

'What about about you, Carl? Where are you heading?'

'To London. Do you want to come?'

Where I really wanted to go was the promised land of Woody Guthrie, Buffalo Bill, John Lee Hooker and Bob Dylan, to wander about in New York, California and Louisiana, but the vast Atlantic ocean lay in my way. Crossing the North sea was easier.

I have often found myself at the right time in the right place and arriving in London in the summer of 1965 was no different. The mid-sixties folk boom was exploding. Jannie and I soon found part-time work in the kitchen of a Hampstead club, although during the months we were in town, we never managed to get a fixed address—spending nights in folk clubs, riding the subway back and forth, trying to keep each other awake in all night diners such as the Chicken Inn, sneaking into the rooms of au pair girls for a shower, sleeping on park benches. My favourite haunt was a folk joint in Soho, *Les Cousins*. It opened at dusk and closed around dawn, the perfect place to spent the night—usually me, wide awake and transfixed, Jannie, asleep, drooling over my shoulder.

The club really was just a small downstairs coffee bar in the basement of a restaurant in Greek street, but in the few months of its existence, it fast became the central hub of the folk scene. Across the Atlantic, in Greenwich Village, New York, it was Bob Dylan, Dave Van Ronk, Fred McNeil, Karen Dalton, Richie Havens, The New Lost City Ramblers and others that caused a musical blooming. In London, guitar explorers like Davy Graham, Bert Jansch and John Renbourn, charismatic songwriters Paul Simon, Al Stewart and Jackson C. Frank, singers Sandy Denny and Long John Baldry transformed the former, often purist, British folk scene and made history. All of them dropped in and out of Les Cousins to perform a set, as if it was their living room.

When Jannie acquired a steady girlfriend, I became a regular night hawk at the club. I was in awe, had a lot to learn. Jackson C. Frank might have been the same age as me, but he was a master, I was a novice. Though I had been writing blues and love songs, guitar tunes with weird titles such as 'Dris Bin Achmed Charhadi Has a Life Full of Holes', inspired by the Lebanese oud players I loved, English was still a language I was mastering. In my Catholic college priority was given to Dutch, French, ancient Latin and Greek. I would have to tramp a zillion miles through mud before I would leave a footprint.

While in the English pubs patrons talked over whoever was performing, at Les Cousins the artists were given full appreciation. Rules were strict. No one talked during performances, unless invited to sing along. During sets, fans were turned off, the front door closed. Coffee was served in the breaks. The anointed king of the castle was Davy Graham, a tall and lean guitarist with a fabulous finger-style technique, creole skin, and a moustache, son of a Gaelic teacher and a woman from Guyana. I only saw him play twice, though he was a regular visitor and his presence was palpable, always a pretty woman by his side. An enigmatic man of few words with an air of mysticism, he could have been a monk, wiry and gaunt like an army officer, a hardcore traveller who busked around France, Greece and North Africa. A maverick musician who experimented with alternative guitar tunings, blended traditional Celtic music with blues, jazz and Arabic scales, an innovator who blew the acoustic guitar world wide open, like Jimi Hendrix would do to the electric guitar later on. He was ahead of everyone else.

For me, who was raised on the global sounds borrowed from the Mechelen record library, Davy Graham was an inspiration that made me rethink everything I had taken for granted and dismantle the walls of possibilities I had constructed for myself. He inspired everyone else too. Every guitar player worth his mint learned to play Davy's guitar piece 'Anji', a tune also recorded by Bert Jansch and Paul Simon (for his *Sound of Silence* album).

Les Cousins was almost a family affair, but Davy was on his own journey. His adoration of Charlie Parker and the jazz improvisors led him to heroin, becoming a junkie by choice and he disappeared from the professional world of music, though his influence was long lasting. I saw him years later at an arena concert in Deurne outside of Antwerp, together with my brother Luc. He was squeezed between the up and coming British rock bands, Fleetwood

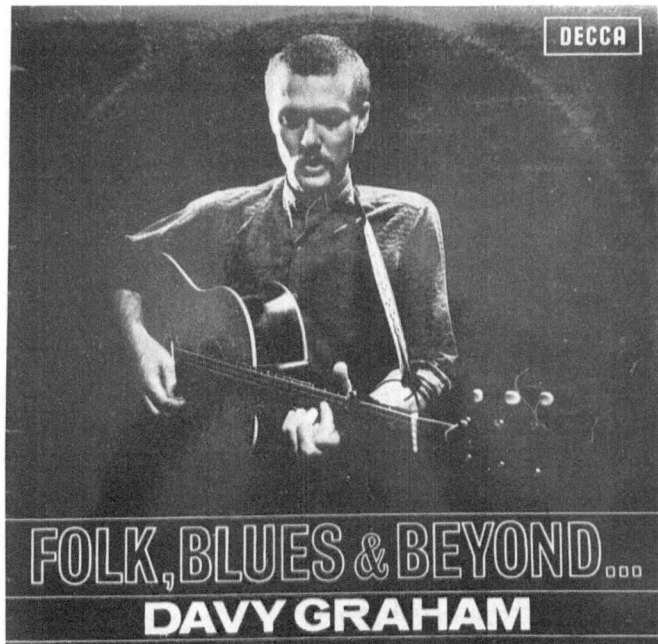
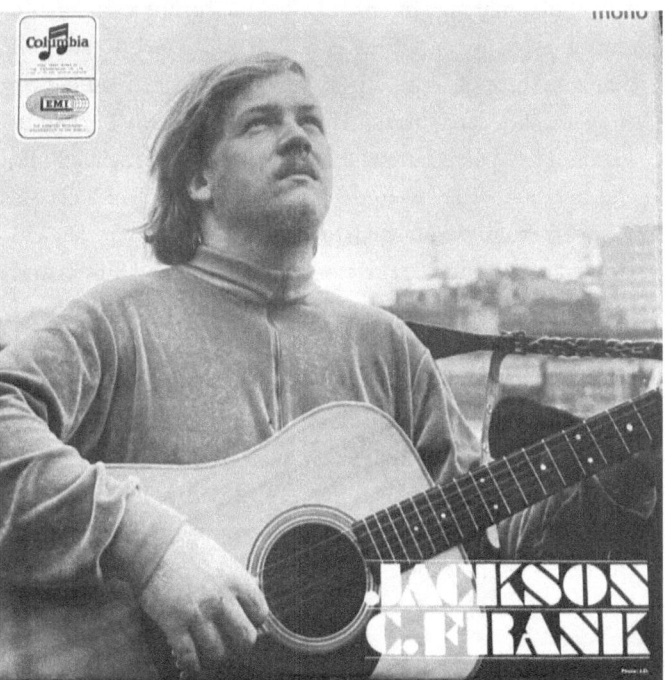

Mac, The Nice, Yes and Colloseum, but Davy's acoustic guitar was inaudible from the stands. I scampered down the stairs and squeezed my way through the crowd to the front of the stage only to arrive as Davy walked off in disgust.

Two Americans, Jackson C. Frank and Paul Simon, were also stand-out regulars at Les Cousins, fine fingerpickers and songwriters who came to England looking for the success that was eluding them at home. Before I ever saw Paul Simon perform I heard a tape of him at someone's loft, where I had my first marihuana experience. I giggled all evening and left with the song 'I am a Rock' wired in my brain. Simon was an impressive songster and fine guitar player, a bit nerdy, a college boy with glasses and a cardigan. Jackson C. Frank had the moustache and the air of a duke, a lover of fancy cars, intense like a Cossack, but friendly, shy and quietly spoken, at times withdrawn. Once I saw him limping through his songs, oblivious to his audience, wrapped in a dark shroud. He was scarred, badly burned in a school fire when he was ten. His songs were melancholic and personal. They went deep within. He too had a classic song every folkie learned to sing and play. Bert Jansch, Donovan and Nick Drake adopted the song and Simon and Garfunkel recorded it. The song was 'Blues Run the Game'. He had written it on the ship that brought him over. Paul Simon, who had recorded a one-hour session of solo recordings for Columbia, titled *The Paul Simon Songbook*, not long before my arrival, brought Jackson to the label where Paul produced his first self-titled solo record. It would be Jackson's only album. He returned to the USA where his somber moods gradually worsened. He was losing his grip on reality, slipped into a personal hell of homelessness, medications, hospitals and mental institutions with the occasional recovery in between. He was king for a brief time, only to vanish, though never forgotten for his one brilliant album. He made songwriters rethink their craft. Jackson C. Frank too was before his time.

One night I mustered up my courage and asked Bert Jansch whether I could sing of couple of songs during his break. Bert was sitting on a sofa in the dark back corner beside the American banjo player Derroll Adams, who wrote the song 'Portland Town', destined to become a traditional folk song. Derroll looked like a Chinese sage, a tall man of undefined age, though he certainly was older than any of us. With his deep warm voice he could pass for your amiable uncle or benevolent grandfather. He had taken young Donovan under his wing. Derroll had come to Europe with Ramblin' Jack Elliott, who styled himself after Woody Guthrie, and when Jack returned to the States Adams remained, eventually settling in Belgium for the rest of his life. When my friend Bebert opened the first folk club in my home town, The Kazoo, we both drove to Antwerp to bring Derroll and his banjo over to inaugurate the club. We bought two small bottles of gin as a bribe to get him to come. It was a good investment.

With Bert and Derroll watching from the back I sang a blues and a ballad I had written and would record a few months later in Germany. The applause was gracious and I returned to the corner stool I had claimed for the night. A curly-haired woman came to sit beside me. She wore a black sweater emblazoned with a large cross. Eccentric, but this was Soho. She told me that she had liked my songs and asked me where I was from and where I was staying. When she found out I had nowhere to stay, she invited me to her home.

We left the club and ambled around Soho. She greeted people as we walked along. Soho is alive at any time of the night. Bars, restaurants, strip clubs, massage parlours, sex cinemas, streetwalkers, hustlers, bohemians. She told little about herself, only that she was Jewish, had fled Germany before the Second World War and was now associated with St Anne's Church in Soho. Judith knew the gang of musicians that hung at the coffee bar well. Jackson and Al Stewart were often staying at her place. Paul was a dear friend. She had written the liner notes for his album. He was staying with her now. We talked music, arts, books, philosophies, the changing times. She was short in stature, but larger than life, a bright intelligence and a big heart who offered her flat in East London as a resting place to the homeless songwriters and lost souls she met around Soho. She had nurtured many.

We took the subway to Shadwell, somewhere in the London docks, chatting all the way, and stayed up all night, sitting on the carpet in her loungeroom, talking softly not to wake the rest of the flat, sipping tea until I could not keep focused and fell asleep on the sofa. Too few hours later I was woken by an American voice. It was Paul Simon, who had lodged in an adjoining room with his girlfriend Katie. He had to rush out to catch a plane to Copenhagen. It had been a fateful day for me. It would be a fateful day for Paul Simon. I only met him briefly that morning. Hello, good luck and goodbye, half asleep. What Paul didn't know then was that, in his absence, the CBS producer Tom Wilson had overdubbed drums, electric bass and guitar, and added an echo chamber effect to 'The Sound of Silence', one of the songs of an album Paul had recorded in the USA with his high school buddy, Art Garfunkel, titled *Wednesday Morning, 3 A.M.* The album had been a flop and the duo had travelled to England in 1965 to try their luck in the blossoming folk circuit. Meanwhile the folk-rock craze had taken over the States. The Byrds hit the charts with an electrified version of Dylan's 'Mr Tambourine Man'. Dylan himself changed the course of musical history with 'Like a Rolling Stone'. Tom Wilson was a smart man. CBS re-released the song to cash in. Paul would find out in Copenhagen. The single topped the US charts on New Year's Day 1966. Paul had to rush back to the USA. Simon and Garfunkel reunited and their career took off. The next time I visited Judith she had a brand new stereo, a thank you from Paul. Judith included me in one of her folk church concerts but soon afterwards I returned to Belgium, first to finish my university degree and then to leave for Africa. Jannie went East to India. Some of us would meet down the track someplace. Others I never saw again.

9
AFRICA

Impossible things happen and inevitable things don't. I did finish my law studies and I did managed to escape from a future that was being planned for me, thanks to a scholarship that would allow me to specialise in International Law in South Africa. To satisfy our families, my on/off girlfriend Beatrice and I got married and we left Belgium the next day on an ocean liner from Amsterdam. It was January 1967. We crossed the equator for the first time, dropped anchor in the Canary Islands, Cape Town, Port Elizabeth, East London and Durban and arrived by rail in Johannesburg, twenty-one days after our departure. We were in for a shock.

While in Western Europe a flowering of all the arts left an indisputable fragrance of wondrous change in the air, in South Africa apartheid, the doctrine of white supremacy and racial segregation, was at the height of vicious state repression. Pass laws, arbitrary arrests, police brutality, banned persons, resettlements—euphemism for forced removals – were the order of the day. An invisible cloak of things unspoken smothered everything. People tried to act with normality but nothing was normal. I had read about it, but it never had seemed quite real. Coming in from the outside, it choked you. Too many questions one could not ask. Ignore the elephant in the room, shackled on four ankles, open wounds of the lash on her flanks?

Everything was segregated: schools, hospitals, transport, toilets, shops, beaches, park benches—even sexual intercourse. The black sections were always inferior. Pettiness reigned. Blacks were not allowed in white cinemas, nor could they buy liquor, only a poor quality government-supplied beer. Blacks could not own land nor start a business in white areas. Paranoia reigned. The Beatles were banned and I remember the clandestine thrill of first hearing *Sgt Pepper's Lonely Heart Club Band* at an artists' party on the banks of the Crocodile River. TV was considered subversive and remained prohibited until 1976. On the poster for the American Western *Sergeants Three*, featuring the Rat Pack celebrities Frank Sinatra, Dean Martin, Sammy Davis Jr., Peter Lawford and Joey Bishop, Sammy's face was covered up so that a black man would not appear besides the white men on the poster. African political parties were forced underground. Mandela was in jail, others had fled. The armed resistance was increasing.

Elsewhere the world was changing. Colonial empires were crumbling. A new generation called for revolution. Students were in rebellion. The summer of love reigned while blacks rioted in Detroit and Washington. Martin Luther King had denounced the Vietnam War; Muhammad Ali refused to fight and was stripped of his titles. The tide was turning. But I only heard of these events on the grapevine. State media were censored. We had landed in a parallel world.

Through a fortunate circumstance I swapped International Law for African Music and became the student of ethnomusicologist Professor John Blacking, dean of the Music and Anthropology Department of Witwatersrand University. Beatrice found work in a pharmacy and embarked on a crash course in English while I spent much of my time on campus or on research outings. Witwatersrand was reputedly the most liberal university in the country but, beside a few Africans in our African studies department and the cleaners, it was white all over—students and staff. There was no open dissent. The politics of blatant injustice were justified or whispered about. For most white folks the African world was inaccessible without permits. Only Africans with a special pass could work in white areas, mostly as servants or labourers.

The Africa that I had dreamt of was elusive. I had no contact with African musicians and there was no African music in Johannesburg to be heard. The only musicians I had bonded with were Indians and we rarely met. Repression hung like asbestos over the place, poisoning everyone. Only a sympathetic Belgian consul and Professor John Blacking provided a crack in the wall. The year spent in South Africa shook me to the core and left me with a lifelong commitment to the struggle against apartheid.

There were only three honour students in John Blacking's African Studies Department: a journalist, an older Dominican priest and me, but I was the only one to accompany John on his outings and attend his parties. I met the journalist twice and the priest, whom I only knew as Father Ten Velde, knocked on my door one morning in the company of a woman, pleading with me to witness their marriage at the City Hall in half an hour's time, since he knew no one else outside his lifelong church community and they, of course, all disapproved.

'We are in hiding', he said.

She smiled apologetically. We had to rush out the door. It was all very romantic. Father Ten Velde was wearing a cheap suit. He had never held 'a proper job'. The church had looked after him. When he had spoken out against the injustices he had been banned from the pulpit. The church too did not want to rock the apartheid boat. Swapping his robes for a wedding ring was the final straw. Mr and Ms Ten Velde were now friendless and destitute. But this was not the moment for gloom. The ceremony was over in minutes and soon we stood back on the pavement, bewildered among the midday traffic. I suggested a celebration. The new husband pointed at a nearby snack bar where I toasted the bride and groom with milkshakes. I never saw them again.

I had few friends, felt isolated, and was grateful to have been taken under the wings of my mentor John Blacking, who provided me with the first glimpses of musical Africa. He was a passionate and charismatic man. His innovative field research among the Venda with extensive notes, recordings, photographs and film footage arguably provided the most complete record of a non-western musical culture amassed up to that time. I would encounter his books in foreign libraries years later. And so, as an academic of stature, he was able to obtain permits to enter 'non-white areas' such as distant Venda and Sotho communities, the Soweto township and the gold mining compounds outside Jo'burg where thousands of young men from all over southern Africa worked six days a week under the migrant labour system, digging in the darkness.

On Sundays a rough wooden amphitheatre provided an arena for the different tribal groupings in turn to stomp their feet on the sand, rattle their ankle bells, chant, dance and march, while others watched and cheered. It was exciting. Power and spirit on display. As the Carole King song goes: 'I feel the earth move under my feet'. But the miners were not free to move, not free to leave the compound during the period of their contracts, not free to wear traditional dress nor play their drums. The living quarters were overcrowded, segregated along tribal lines for fear of revolt. They were indentured labourers. Many were beaten, shackled and abused by foremen or killed in accidents.

John and I watched the spectacle for a while, then took our field recorder outside where all around the men continued dancing up the dust and singing for hours after their performance. I guess there was little else for them to do. Some of them showed off their prowess slapping their hands and rubber gumboots in fast rhythms, thumping the earth. There was much ground water down in the shafts and the mining executives thought it cheaper to give the workers boots than draining floors. Down there they were forbidden to speak and learned to communicate by slapping their boots. That is how the gumboot dance originated in those gold mines. It became a form of entertainment. These men were a long way from home in tough circumstances.

As for John, outspoken and stubborn, he always walked the thin line of defiance, until a year later he was declared persona non grata and expelled from South Africa.

I was not ready to fly straight back into a hornets' nest of bourgeois expectations. By now, obsessed with all-things African, I wanted to make my way back to Europe overland. I was in no hurry at all. And neither was Beatrice. Aroused by the free winds of the sixties we would hitchhike, bus, truck or walk from Johannesburg, across the African continent to the Mediterranean sea. No planes. 'When I was a boy, I always saw myself as a hero in comic books and in movies. I grew up believing this dream,' Elvis Presley once said. Likewise I longed to impersonate my Tintin and Tarzan fantasies, while following my musical obsessions on the back roads of Africa, and Beatrice followed me—both of us happy to be away from small town Mechelen.

With the collapse of colonialism Africa was undergoing a turbulent time of revolutionary change. It was an exhilarating moment in its history. Newly independent countries were born, civil wars and wars of liberation fought, massive social and political make-overs were taking place. Expectations were high. Obstacles precipitous. Africa was an enormous distraction for a Flemish ex-boy scout. Wildlife still ran free, though the gradual slaughter would soon escalate. Most of the continent was rural then, well before the age of the megacities. And Africa is the cradle of music. The rest of the planet and weighty considerations of future clock-on times could wait.

We recouped our return flights to Belgium and set out north to follow the jungle line across the continent. It became a journey that would occupy almost a year. We would remain off the radar for weeks at a time in that pre-digital era, receiving belated news of the assassination of Robert Kennedy, the May Day street battles in Paris and the death of Che Guevara in Bolivia. Students occupied universities while Beatrice and I tossed and turned on the roof of a truck in Zululand, dodging a hyena that ransacked our supplies. Race riots set American cities ablaze while we were trapping antelopes in a remote part of northern Uganda*. The six-day war between the Arabs and the Israelis had just been fought when we arrived in Cairo, the sandbags and military still positioned in front of government buildings and banks. Somehow we missed the death of Martin Luther King. If Africa was in turmoil, so was the rest of the world. Something was happening, mister Jones. The world was rocking under the king tides of change and in the midst of all this violent upheaval a generation sprouted a revolutionary seed of a spirit prone to questioning and experimentation. It was exciting to be alive.

At the start of it all, one sunny morning, Beatrice and I hitchhiked out of Johannesburg, passed Pretoria before midday and headed north to the Zimbabwean border. Zimbabwe was still called Rhodesia then, an ex-British colony that in 1965 had declared independence from its colonial master. Like its neighbour, South Africa, the white minority

---

*as told in *Tarab, Travels with my Guitar* (Transit Lounge Publishing)

had established a white supremacist government. Like the rulers in Pretoria, the Rhodesian government of Ian Smith believed it was defending Western values against a backward race, preserving Christianity, fighting communism, fighting for survival. Even today, some still try to sell us that notion. It was the official doctrine and for most of the white population a good enough excuse, a blindfold against the obvious injustice. In Rhodesia it was Robert Mugabe who was imprisoned without trial and both African opposition parties, ZAPU and ZANU, had begun campaigns of guerrilla warfare. They considered themselves freedom fighters against oppression and racial discrimination, while the white government saw them as terrorists. An all too familiar story.

The border guards were suspicious and unwelcoming. Was I a communist? Travelling to Zambia? Overland? With backpacks and a guitar? Were we crazy? There was a war going on. Our acquaintances in Johannesburg had admonished us that an overland journey through the continent was a dangerous and foolish idea. Since African countries began gaining independence from their European colonial masters, much of the news in the closed and censured white society was focused on these countries where trouble had broken out, an obvious sign that the Africans were incapable of self-governing. The white settlers from Rhodesia and South Africa lived in an ivory tower, unable to visit the rest of the continent because of their government's racist policies. We were given a six-day transit visa, walked two hundred meters down the road and waited for a vehicle that might take us to Bulawayo.

Past Bulawayo, through northern Ndebele country, there was hardly any traffic at all. It was slow going. All our rides were with the army. Our last lift to Victoria Falls was a bumpy ride in the back of a truck with South African soldiers who were here to give the Rhodesians a helping hand. They were all rural boys from the Transvaal, machine guns on their knees, laughing and full of bravura, as if they were out on a boy scout excursion.

'Let's give these kaffirs a lesson!' they yelled, stopping the truck along the banks of the Zambezi River and firing their machine guns into Zambia for our benefit. The next day we crossed the bridge over Victoria Falls into Zambia.

The Smith government eventually collapsed. International sanctions, guerillas at their door and a white exodus broke their resolve to continue the fight. Military defeat was certain. Majority rule came to Zimbabwe in 1980 with Robert Mugabe as the first president.

Beatrice and I zigzagged north haltingly through an obstacle course, from Zambia, to Malawi and Tanzania. The Rhodesian war caused serious petrol shortages in the region and thus, few trucks. Border soldiers in the rural outposts of the new nations were unfamiliar with the sight of a dust-covered white couple with a guitar and backpacks. The white masters had just left and, all of them had jeeps and cars. They did not travel on foot.

'We must phone the capital in Zomba to get clarifications.'

'But we have been here two days now. Why are you not calling?'

'Because the wind is not right.'

But, in the end, this was Africa then. There was always a village nearby, curious people finding us on deserted roads, inviting us in, or keeping us company during the endless hours of waiting in the shade of an acacia tree for a truck or bus that might come today or tomorrow. A guitar, or any instrument, is a great facilitator when one does not share the language. Even more so in Africa, where music is embedded in every aspect of life, work and culture.

I did not hear any music during our short stay in Zimbabwe and have never returned since we crossed that bridge, but in 1993 the Bhundu Boys, Zimbabwe's most successful band, toured Australia, and the Hottentot Party—the band I had founded with Greek-Australian singer Parissa Bouas—was invited to open the show for them. I was thrilled. Their jit style of dance music with its rippling electric guitars, bouncy bass, syncopated beat and call-and-response vocals in the Shona language was the most joyous, infectious music I had heard. It made you smile. It made you move.

They had arrived in England during the mid-eighties and found instant success. Everyone loved the Bhundus. Madonna invited them to play as her support act at the Wembley stadium. The recording giant Warner Music signed them. But the band we met wasn't smiling. They sat sullen in the dressing room, not interested in small talk. There was no dancing on stage. They went through the motions. The joy went missing. 'That Lismore's Hottentot Party should play with more inspiration than Zimbabwe's Bhundu Boys was another achievement for local music,' wrote reviewer Paul Shaw in The Northern Star. But there was more to the story.

The happiness that this band had once emanated had turned to sorrow and tragedy. Between 1991 and 1993 the keyboard player and the original bassist, as well as his replacement, all died from Aids. Bad management, wrong producers and infighting among the band hastened the downfall. The charismatic frontman and main songwriter, Biggie Tembo, was asked to leave the band. The Bhundu Boys had named themselves after the young boys who used to aid the guerrilla fighters as messengers and lookouts in the war against the white minority government. Biggie Tembo had been a Bhundu boy. He wrote the great songs and animated the audience. Tembo never recovered from his expulsion from the band and would hang himself in a Harare asylum in 1995. His penniless widow ended up cleaning toilets at a beer hall in Harare. The band didn't recover either. For all the joy they brought the world, the Bhundu Boys would be remembered as the Band that died of Aids.

10

HIPPIES AND REFUGEES

uring my two years hiding out in Africa I missed the birth of hippiedom and all those psychedelic bands that exploded during the American summer of love of 1967. I was as unaware of all the goings on between troubadours in the hills around Laurel Canyon as I was ignorant of the epic happenings that rocked the world during the late sixties. Browsing through old copies of Time magazine when collecting mail at an Embassy in Kampala or Khartoum, I learned that, in my absence, the Prague Spring had been crushed by the Soviets, the Vietnam war had expanded, massacres were common now, while resistance against the war and racism had grown into militancy. In France a student uprising erupted, the Beatles stopped performing and astronauts walked on the moon. So much had happened and I needed to catch up.

Beatrice and I rented a flat in the harbour city of Antwerp at the beginning of sixty-nine. The revolt in nearby Paris had fizzled, Mao Zedong's Cultural Revolution was pumping and Richard Nixon had taken up the presidency. There was a restless feeling in the air, more change and upheaval than people could bear. Africa had been in a different time zone, where watches and calendars were meaningless. Each day was just another day. Anchored in the present. The best way to live. Within weeks Beatrice and I were joined in our one-bedroom flat by my three South African buddies, Maurice, Amin and Omar, all stateless refugees from the apartheid regime, whom I had befriended in Nairobi where they were stuck in limbo, embroiled in a tussle between two countries. The men camped out in our lounge room and we slept in the bedroom down the hall, with the bathroom in between. They all had a turbulent past, wanted men in their own country, trained as guerrilla fighters in the former Yugoslavia and sent back to Africa to fight the Rhodesian and South African white supremacy regimes. Suicidal incursions were common, especially when international bodies discussed funds for the African National Congress. I have told their story in my book *Tarab—Travels with my Guitar*. In Kenya these men had taken Beatrice and I under their wing when we had run into some strife and I had been able to return the favour by, somehow, through connections within the Belgian Embassy in Nairobi, obtaining them a refugee permit for residence with us in Belgium. However, the bureaucracy involving refugee papers from the UN officials, hesitant Belgian diplomats and paranoid security agents, wary of these military men trained in a communist country, was plodding, crawling and dragging on. It took them another six months to arrive on our doorstep in the Lange Lozanastraat in Antwerp while Beatrice and I made our way home through Uganda, the Sudan, Egypt, Lybia, Tunisia and Algeria where we boarded a ship across the Mediterranean sea to Marseille and hitched north to Flanders in the December freeze of 1968.

And so the psychedelic rage of Californian bands largely passed me by. Leonard Cohen had caught my attention with his songs 'Suzanne' and 'So Long, Marianne', and so did Joni Mitchell, two Canadians who were like a synthesis of the French Chansonniers and the American folk wave. Joni Mitchell especially blew me away. Her melodies and guitar stylings were more innovative than anyone else around. She was impossible to ignore, a lyricist to match Dylan and Cohen. She was belatedly given her proper due by a male dominated rock industry, but she certainly was one of the finest songwriters in the English language of the twentieth century.

With my brother Luc, ten years younger than me, a fine lad of sixteen now, I went prowling the local record shops for what was new and he introduced me to some of the emerging bands coming out of England: Yes, Fleetwood Mac, Jethro Tull, Led Zeppelin, Pink Floyd, King Crimson. We had not spent much time together before, and it was a thrill to see these bands with him and hang out. My bohemian friends in Mechelen and Antwerp turned me on to Frank Zappa, a musical genius in his own right. The sweet harmonies and songs of Crosby, Stills and Nash caught my fancy as well. All of these artists were cutting new trails through the jungle world of popular music. But my main focus, sharing a small space with my restless South African brothers, was pulled towards the political world and their own precarious future. I was doing uninteresting jobs to get by, hardly touching my guitar. It had a dramatic ending for all us all and by the end of 1970 our world disintegrated.* A few weeks later Beatrice and I set out eastward and, with my departure, my soundtracks too changed. I would not return for twelve years.

---

*the story is told in *Tarab. Travels with my guitar* (Transit Lounge Pub 2008/2014)

11
INDIA

My journey to India began when I was three years old, the year the Belgian magazine Tintin, was founded, a publication that was a milestone in my life and, I would guess, for all the young of heart in Belgium and France. It heralded the blossoming of the Belgo-French comic strips that would grow flowers, orchards and vineyards for decades to come. A flowering akin to the golden age of Pieter Breugel and Jeroen Bosch, the Flemish and Dutch Renaissance masters, five hundred years before. Tintin magazine featured a range of heroes in weekly ongoing adventures that took place in different eras and countries. Corentin was a favourite. The artwork of its author, Paul Cuvelier, was superb. Corentin was an orphan boy in Brittany during the eighteenth century. He flees a drunken and abusive uncle as a stowaway on a ship. After being attacked by pirates he shipwrecks on the coast of India. I probably was reading the tale -first the pictures, then the words – when Jawaharlal Nehru raised the national flag of independence above the Lahori Gate of the Red Fort in Delhi in August 1947. Corentin was my first glimpse of India, albeit of two centuries ago, a boy's India with a sultan and a princess, tigers and evil priests. Religious pomp with parades of painted elephants. I put it on my 'adventures: to do' list.

At high school I developed a taste for Indian music, thanks to my town's record library. The classical ragas fired my reveries more than the Gregorian chants at Catholic school. I had also developed a crush on the female singers who, whatever their age, always sounded like young girls, and rigged up an echo system in my bedroom—recording the LP on my reel to reel and playing it back with a slight delay to the disc – to let the songbirds serenade me from the top of the Himalayas, unaware of my mother yelling from two storeys downstairs: 'Can you turn it down please!'

A few weeks after my arrival in Johannesburg I had a fateful meeting with Rodney Jacobs at an Indian classical dance performance. Rodney was one of the dancers. He was an Afrikaner, a gay man and a dancer of Indian music in a racist, white, and segregated country. He was small in stature, cultured and sensitive, perhaps too sensitive for the times. I liked him instantly and he would become one of my best friends. Rodney did not make a difference between day and night and would drop by at any crazy hour. Instead of sleeping he survived on catnaps. It was Rodney who introduced me to Jeram, an Indian sitarist who lived in Benoni on the outskirts of Jo'Burg. Together we formed a trio with a tabla player. But, though it was fun for a while, we only managed to perform once, at a concert at university. Rehearsals were difficult to arrange and performances even more so. Indians were classified as coloureds and Benoni was a good distance from my flat in Hillbrow. One night when Jeram stayed overnight, neighbours dobbed him in and the police came. Under the Immorality Act different races could not sleep under the same roof.

India found us again in Kenya, this time through the Sikh community of bus drivers, mechanics, engineers, policemen, shopkeepers, sawmillers and farmers. Reliable men in a unstable time. The first Indians to East Africa were brought over by the British colonial power at the end of the 19th century to lay 576 kilometres of railway tracks through hot arid country, from Mombasa on the Indian Ocean, up to the highlands, ten thousand feet high, and down into the Great Rift valley to Lake Victoria. Most of these labourers were Sikhs from the Punjab. It was a perilous undertaking. For every mile of railway line laid four men died. Others were eaten by lions. After the job was done many returned to India, but some seven thousand remained and more would follow.

By the mid-sixties, when independence came to the new nations of Tanzania, Kenya and Uganda, there was a network of Sikhs in place. From bullock carts to trucks and busses, stations and garages, they had a handle on transport from the start and that was a great help to us. Once we had befriended one Sikh we were often passed on to others for lodging or bus and truck rides on the journeys ahead between Dar Es Salaam and Kigali and north towards the Sudanese border. Sikhs became like the uncle you could depend on when you were stuck someplace. The turbans and beards gave them a certain nobility, an air of the Knights of the Round Table. They were willing to help, offer solutions and their cuisine was a welcome respite from the rough bush meat and bananas along the roads of Africa.

Beatrice and I were standing beneath the viaduct on the Neckerspoel at the outskirts of Mechelen hitching a ride. It was January the 4th, 1971 and it had been snowing all night, a porridge of sludge was freezing over. Now and then a train rumbled above us, on its way to Antwerp or Brussels. We were both wrapped in several jumpers, scarves and jackets, thick socks and boots. A grey Citroen stopped beside us.

'Where are you going?'

'To India.'

'You have chosen a good day. Step inside.'

We were dropped beside the road on the outskirts of Leuven. It was snowing again. By nightfall we were squeezed in the front seat cabin with two Turkish truck drivers heading for Munich.

A polar cold air swept over Europe during the winter of '71. Temperatures sank as we drove deeper into the continent. Minus 28 at the Austrian border. Yugoslavia lay like a frozen ocean, villages and farmsteads sunk deep in snow, smoke puffing out of chimneys like periscopes. All of Turkey was blanketed, the roads hazardous with a veneer of frozen snow, the narrow mountain passes east of Erzurum throttled, truck drivers hacking and digging out blocks of ice in the glacial night. We crossed Iran from west to east to a cheerless Afghan border post, forsaken in a wind-swept, desolate expanse. Iran was still ruled by an emperor and Afghanistan by a king. Zahir Shah had ruled the country since he was nineteen, when his father was assassinated in 1933. The Soviet invasion was eight years away, the mujahideen wars and the rise of the Taliban still to come. The US invasion and its defeat by the same Taliban came five decades after my time there. Who could have foreseen the tragic future of Afghanistan then?

Beatrice and I, bundled in layers of army disposal garb beneath Afghan sheep coats, both naive and wide-eyed on our first incursion into the heart of Asia, were cast into a pre-industrial era of peasants, warlords and codes, a medieval time of heroism, honour, religious rigidity and tribal allegiance, like travellers in H.G. Wells's Time Machine. We had straggled through Africa from south to north, but nothing had prepared us for this. Gaudy trucks –a kaleidoscope of mirrors and flamboyant paintings— carried us through bleak and dusty landscapes on the few roads, built with US and Soviet aid, from Herat south to the Pathan heartland and the ancient capital Kandahar, and on to Kabul. There was little traffic, camels more prevalent than horses or cars. Much of the country was suffering a catastrophic drought and almost three-quarters of the nation's sheep, the main meat staple, had perished. Some were eating their horses, others fled into Pakistan and Iran in search of food. The winter was merciless. There was an unfamiliar fierceness about these people. Many men were armed, often with ancient rifles, women invisible behind burqas. We had no language in common. Contact with Afghani women was minimal. The men were hospitable and courteous. But for them we were curious, infidel travellers who belonged to another world.

'Why was I here?' they asked. 'Were we pilgrims? Businessmen?'

We travelled down the Khyber Pass into Pakistan and arrived, ten days later, at the Indian border, three months after our departure. I finally had come to the country whose music had given me so much rapture. Since our travels through East Africa Sikhs had felt like family, so when Beatrice and I entered India our first destination was the city of Amritsar, capital of the Punjab.

We sold all our winter clothing, sleeping bags and boots on the pavement, surrounded by a curious crowd, while one of countless tailers with a sewing machine stitched us cotton kurtas and pyjamas. Inching through the streets of Amritsar, congested with pilgrims, mendicants and vendors we shuffled to the most important shrine of Sikhism, the Golden Temple, a large complex built around a man-made pool during the sixteenth century, destroyed time and time again—by the Mughal and Afghan invaders and, most recently—thirteen years after our visit—under Indira Gandhi who, as revenge, was in turn assassinated by her Sikh body guards. The powerful can command everything, save their own destiny. But each time the temple was rebuilt. It is the religion's principle gurdwara, or palace of worship.

We made a clockwise circumambulation around the pool that fed us on to a causeway in a stream of devotees and into the sanctum, glittering in the centre of the lake in the late afternoon sun. White marble floors. Copperplated walls. A dome of gold foil. Inside, the sacred scriptures lay on a raised platform while a man sang kirtans and prayers, accompanying himself on a harmonium. Even though a crowd of worshippers passed through, everyone was filled with a calm serenity. We lingered. This was my first experience, however brief, of meditating, enveloped in kirtan song. It was a call from another life. Many of our Sikh friends in Uganda had never visited their holiest shrine and my heart was with them. No one expected that, a few years later, Idi Amin would evict them and steal their homes. Exiting the sanctum each one of us was handed a sweet offering and in the evening a vegetarian meal was served in a gigantic kitchen. Sikhism is a tolerant creed. Food is served to all visitors who want it, regardless of faith, while sharing and service to the community is recommended to overcome egotism. We even slept in the temple complex that night.

Whereas in the homes of my Sikh friends in East Africa I had mostly been exposed to Bollywood film songs I now got to appreciate the real devotional kirtan songs that lie at heart of Sikh music. Sikhs believe that music is the best way to absorb the scriptures and to express devotion. Singing the kirtans is a spiritual act. The musical hymns of their Holy Book, the Granth Sahib, are based on the raags of the ancient Hindustani Classical tradition with its complex structured scales and rules. The Granth Sahib is the world's largest body of sacred songs and it comprises a total of sixty ragas. In the modern day gurdwaras the hymns are performed during worship in a slow and steady hypnotising manner, usually backed by the harmonium and tablas, whereas in the time of Guru Nanak, the founder of Sikkhism, five hundred years earlier, string instruments were used. Finding occasional refuge and kirtan peace in gurdwaras was a gift during my year in the country, until my very last days, when the Calcutta gurdwara sheltered Beatrice and I from the madness of the Bangla Desh Independence war, only kilometres away, and the nightly blackouts and panic that enveloped the city. It was our first and our last haven in the country that was expelling us.

India, its contemplative music and its manifold culture, opened a path into introspection. The meditative states and its practical codes to live by, offered by Buddhism, Sikkhism, Hinduism, Jainism and Taoism, gently untangled the gnarled coil of religious dogmatism stitched into me from birth. I had one more meeting with God in a dream, when I caught him peeking through my keyhole. He was in his traditional garb, with a grey beard and a long white robe. He could have passed for Dumbledore or Gandalf, but I recognised him as the peeping creeping Tom with his frocked entourage obsessed with guilt, sex, sin and hellfire, who tormented me throughout my childhood and said:

Hey man, what's going on here?

I am checking up on you.

Why?

To see if you are behaving yourself, doing the right thing.

Who told you to do that?

I am God.

So? That is what they all say. Why don't you bugger off.

No one tells God to bugger off!

Alright, let's have a duel then, I said and brought out two rapiers.

We saluted each other. 'En Garde!' And I pierced him right through the chest. He disappeared in a puff of smoke and I haven't heard from him since.

One of my motives to travel to India, was to work for an NGO in Andhra Pradesh. I had been gripped by the talk of its director, professor Windey, one evening in Antwerp. Two thousand villages had been destroyed by a cyclone in one of the poorest regions of India. Windey had a vision and needed help. I had told him that I would be on my way, but it would take time for me to get there. Half a year after my promise, we made it to Andhra Pradesh. Some of the villages were not easily accessible, and virtually cut-off during the monsoon rains when dry riverbeds suddenly overflowed and all the tracks turned to mud. The agreement was that villagers themselves would build their own dwellings—every man, woman and child—while the organisation designed the plans, provided cement, tools and know-how.

Beatrice helped out in the main office in Guntur while I was designated to the village of Kammavaripalem. There was little to eat, and little to drink. There were no such things as shops. Supplies were brought in from a long distance by truck through dry riverbeds. It was a race against time and everyone laboured seven days per week. It was only weeks before the coming of the monsoon and the wells were reduced to fetid pools. I came down with hepatitis and ended up in a hospital in Guntur, nurtured by Catholic nuns. A few months later I caught hepatitis for a second time during a meditation course in a Buddhist monastery in Bodh Gaya.

By the time I arrived in Kathmandu I was in a poor state and put on to a drip in a small hotel room by a travelling Chinese doctor, Yung Khan, to whom I am forever grateful. An American friend brought me a tiny transistor radio and for two months it lay on my pillow next to my head, tuned into the classical programmes of All India Radio in a ceaseless flow of slow-burn ragas that triggered the trance receptors in my brain, leaving me blissed out and tranquil. I meditated to the deep voices of the Vedas, the perpetual drone of the tampura, the sonorities of the sarangi, the sitar and the violin, the bellowed funk of the south Indian veena, the mallets daintily hammering, like tiptoeing ballerinas, across the hundred strings of the santoor. The breathtaking musicianship surpassed everything I had heard before. I never tired of it. Could have laid there forever. In hindsight, what was a suffering experience of recovery is remembered for its serenity and musical imprints. Music should not be a distraction. It requires total surrender to savour its rewards. Its teaching, nurturing, empowering, its release, is not a given. Otherwise silence is preferable.

Of all the soundtracks of my life Indian music has been the most enduring one, yet I have not returned to the country. In the time that has passed since, India has transformed itself from an agrarian nation to a capitalist consumer society and more than doubled its population. The bullocks that pulled the cart of my destiny took me somewhere else. But I wish to honour and thank all the wonderful Indian musicians that give me so much. And especially, the many female singers, Lakshmi Shankar, Radjulari Aliakbar Khan,

Kishori Amonkar, Kidushi Veena Sahasrabuddhe, Apoorva Gokhale, Ashwini Bhide Deshpande, and Kaushiki Chakraborty, who is named after a goddess who killed two demons and whose voice tames mine every time.

12
ROBBIE BASHO

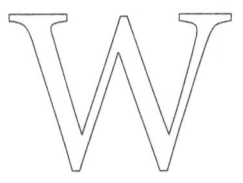aking up early to go to work does not come naturally to me, a reluctance engraved in my DNA after many a glacial Belgian winter's morning, rushed out of my warm bed at 6.40 am to run, shivering in my school shorts, to the Church of Our Lady Across The River Dijle (yes, that is its name), to attend a daily mass imposed by my Catholic college on its victims. This gothic icebox has stood proudly in the Flemish town of Mechelen since the 14th century, though it was burned down once and bombed twice in both world wars. Now that it is all cleaned up -an altar with a modern touch, a carillon with forty nine chimes and colourful windows that pour in a dazzling kaleidoscope of colours in the late afternoon- it stands empty of worshippers. A funeral once in a while, a wedding, a tour of sightseers that stare at the many images of the famous virgin, the stations of the cross and the piece de resistance, a painting by Rubens, none of which impressed me as an altar boy on those freezing mornings.

But by the year 1973, and several rebirths later, things had changed as I sauntered merrily each morning from my communal house in East Balmain, on the Sydney harbourside, to board a ferry that chuffed beneath the Harbour Bridge to Circular Quay from where I stumped along George Street to my job at Peterson, the city's largest music shop. Standing on the deck, breathing in the salty air over the spread of shimmering water, the bobbing boats, the seagulls, the wide open Australian sky and the sharp light bouncing off the white sail-shaped shells of the Opera House, what better way to go to work could there be? Others, less fortunate commuters, sat grim and yawning in overcrowded buses and congested traffic, inhaling diesel smoke and cigarettes.

My Aussie friend John, who had found me penniless in Batu Ferringhi, on the coast of Penang, then still a peaceful village of fishermen and small dwellings, unspoiled yet by the monstrosities of high rise hotels facing polluted waters, had played me a cassette of Cat Stevens and lent me the money to keep travelling on to the Antipodes. I had arrived in Darwin after an eighteen month overland trip from Europe, hitched to Sydney and instantly found a job in a six-storey music emporium in the very heart of the city's CBD, a palace of instruments, records, pianos, sheet music, and a haven for 'temporarily-out-of-work' musicians. I had settled into a routine after years of travel. I was single again.

At that time pub rock ruled Australia and my first introduction was a concert at the Hordern Pavilion with Daddy Cool, a satirical rock band with gutsy songs, peppered with a dash of Frank Zappa's zaniness, that deserved international recognition. I now became acquainted with the songs of the Eagles, Jackson Browne, Stevie Wonder and James Taylor, common in the record cabinet of any communal house, and filled my songbooks with chord charts and lyrics, singing 'Desperado', 'Fire and Rain' and 'Superstition'. Fifty years on and settled back in Australia, I can still walk into a pub or club in any town and hear these songs performed. Fine music never dies.

My life was filled with songs and new friends, and I would often return from work to a dinner, a party or a jam session. There were five of us in the house: three girls, Robert and me. Robert was my co-worker at the shop, a songwriter and guitarist like me. Together we would record most evenings on his reel-to-reel tape deck while downstairs the girls entertained the nightly visitors, drawn to a friendly house with music and charming women. On my way to the ferry I was used to stepping over sleeping guests, left in the lounge room from the night before. One of them, a poet called Bruce, stayed for months and, when we finally had to move, he looked so forlorn that we took him with us.

One evening, a tall and eccentric lad, named Craig, turned up with two records by an American guitarist, Robbie Basho. Joints were shared and everyone sat around on cushions ready to listen, as was a custom of the times. A new album by Led Zeppelin, John Lennon, Curtis Mayfield or Neil Young was celebrated as a major event. Vinyl releases were less common and music was appreciated and not freely available on Spotify or blasted out of every store. Sadly that custom of attentive, and stoned, group listening has disappeared.

With the lights dimmed and incense burning, Craig passed the cover around of the *Song of the Stallion*. It featured a winged white horse flying high above a dark mountain, piercing through a cloudy sky into a patch of clear blue. Craig dropped the needle on to the disc and from the opening strike on Robbie's twelve steel-string guitar we rode into the drama of Basho's world, seated on his stallion like an ancient warrior parading before his sun king. Stately, dignified, pure of heart. The horse trotted. The horse cantered. Guitar arpeggios quickened and tumbled. The horse's hooves galloped in time, lifted off the grass of the steppe and rose. Its golden wings unfurled, its flanks sweating ivory, and as the stallion flew above the mountains and the prairies Robbie Basho's voice erupted without warning, a clarion loud and majestic. It swiftly swelled and soared, exalted and triumphant.

We all looked at each other in disbelief, not knowing whether to laugh or shiver. No one sang like this! This wasn't cool. It is easy to mock a beautiful thing on a wavelength you do not possess. And Basho sang from a mountain of his own, in a century of his own, the child of an Aramaic cantor and the Peruvian coloratura soprano Yma Sumac. Basho descended from another planet, an alien visitor who fell to earth in the wrong century. I had not heard anything like it.

I listened to both albums in wonder. The sound of 12 steel strings in an open tuning never sounded so heavenly. Some of us were mesmerised, other found it all too much, too heavy and esoteric, especially if you were used to the Eagles or Cat Stevens. Basho offered us American ragas, celestial prayers, sacramental medicine, magnificent incantations and monumental visions of thunder and fire, teepees and the princess of the silver water. He blew all expectations out of the water, questioned every preconception and rule of beauty and fashion. The word idiosyncratic was invented for Robbie Basho. You had to abandon your cynicism to fly on his wings to wherever he guided you, abandon all insincerity, jump off the cliff and dive deep. Like a deer or a hawk, he was not here to please.

After my pleading Craig left the records with me—but only for two days—and I spun those four vinyl sides over and over, intoxicated and inspired, while Basho sang of Indian tribes and chiefs, his voice as possessed, once solemn, then bursting into wild yodels, bleating, howling and whistling. He gave me permission. He gave me courage. The second album, *The Voice of the Eagle*, was just as otherworldly. This time a golden eagle ruled the blue sky, hovering above a mountain peak of ice, wings stretched high, positioned to take its prey, the circle of the sun around him, the clouds banished below. I would not see those covers again until the time of the pandemic.

Over the years I made attempts to find his music without any luck. It seemed that Robbie Basho had simply vanished. I did learn that he had died during a chiropractic treatment that burst an artery in 1986 at the age of forty-six. All of his albums were out of print by then. His LPs had never sold more than a few hundred copies and record companies had lost interest. His last work appeared on cassette for the New Age market. He left us with a mystery.

Until, almost half a century later, owners of his rare albums began sharing them on YouTube. Galvanised I spent many a night in wonder, and, this time, my internet searches dug up an interview, a documentary film by Liam Baker and a TV performance of the man who had passed away many years before. Mesmerised I watched a rather chubby guy in a suit, white shirt and tie, wavy hair, a moustache and glasses, looking like an office worker or an insurance salesman in an era when hippies and flower power ruled, step out in front of the cameras on KQED TV. The year was 1971 and he co-starred with the French mime artist Marcel Marceau, an incongruous pairing. The presenter struggled to pronounce the title of his first instrumental piece 'Cathedrals et Fleur de Lis' as Robbie, hunched over his twelve string guitar and totally absorbed, performed his inaccessible but wondrous piece to a puzzled audience. After polite, but confused, clapping, Robbie introduced his next tune.

'I would like to dedicate this music to the avatar Meher Baba and I want to close with a Japanese sonata 'Kowaka De Amour', and within minutes the programs credits appeared and Basho never again faced the camera.

Gradually my digging unravelled the enigma of Robbie Basho like a box of Russian Matryoshka dolls. Born in Baltimore in 1940, orphaned as an infant, his name unknown, adopted as Daniel R. Robinson Jr, he began, as so many other folk guitarists of the time, singing Kingston trio and blues songs, but soon moved to Ravi Shankar ragas, classical Persian, American Indian and Oriental music. He became a student of Ali Akbar Khan, the master of the sarod, and renamed himself after the seventeenth century Japanese poet Matsuo Bashō of whom he believed he was the reincarnation. He invented his own guitar technique and esoteric tunings under the motto 'vision first, technique second' and played the piano like a Persian santoor. As his taste changed, so did his clothes and we see him on his album covers in embroidered dressing gowns, tassled mocassins, a fur hat. Robbie was noticed by John Fahey, another experimental guitarist, who signed him to his guitar label Takoma Records but, though he was an idol to the other guitarists, his records never sold. He was mocked and eventually dumped from the company as well as from the Vanguard and Windham Hill labels.

The story goes that he suffered from a bad LSD trip after which he joined, and perhaps was rescued by, a spiritual group in San Francisco, 'Sufism Reoriented' that worshipped the Indian sage Meher Baba as the avatar, or the manifestation of God, and urged abstaining from drugs and sex. He saw Ivy Duce, the leader of the Sufi group, as his spiritual mother and perhaps she saved him from a downward spiral.

God and music were Basho's raison d'être. They brought him solace and peace. Unlike the rest of his contemporaries, his music was 'not far-out, but far-in'. It was shamanistic. Spirit music. He was not a part of any scene, a loner, a mystic, an oddball, a timeless explorer on the path of beauty. Robbie was not of this earth. He was a shy man, lacked confidence and struggled with loneliness. He never had a driver's licence and was probably still a virgin when he died. On stage he was prone to conversations with beings unseen. To me he was a genius who transported me on angel wings. Music was Basho's exaltation and his intensity, eloquence, dignity, vitality, force, raw emotion, ecstatic yearning and spiritual nobility left its mark.

13

DOLLAR BRAND

In Nimbin, May 1973, eight hundred kilometres north of Sydney, Australia's own Woodstock, the Aquarius festival, took place. I had just turned thirty. All of my house mates in Balmain squeezed into a kombi van and we drove to Nimbin in the lush hinterland of the north coast of New South Wales, a village of dairy farmers and banana growers in rapid decline. We rolled into the one-horse town like Rex, King of the Mardi Gras, in the midst of a festive crowd high on merry flower power. Strangers hugged the new arrivals, offered us joints. The facades in the main street were all painted with flamboyant psychedelic designs by artist-activist, Benny Zable. From the roof of a building a tight-rope walker traipsed above our heads across the street, then wheeled the return journey on a unicycle. It was Philippe Petit, a Frenchman who, in later years, became famous when he walked a cable stretched high up between the Twin Towers, well before the Saudis hit them with highjacked planes. In the small park, where the main street forks, the White Company, a swashbuckling theatre and music ensemble, hammed it up. The fragrance of marihuana wafted through the town. I had landed in a circus, it seemed, a fairyland, a film set.

Expectation hung in the air. A conservative, semi-colonial country, known for its White Australia policy, a nation that tried to erase its history with the blood of its massacres had elected Gough Whitlam, a progressive prime minister and, overnight, the former reactionary state donned a new gown like a college queen at a year twelve formal. Suddenly Australia acquired the golden aura of a promised land. Radical changes were taking place. The soldiers exited Vietnam. Conscription was abolished, universal health care and free university education were implemented. China was recognised. A new future was in store. Or so it seemed in the year of 1973.

But, while the Woodstock festival focused on rock music, the ten-day long Aquarius festival had a broader aim. It celebrated alternative lifestyles, a connection with the land, a counter-culture focusing on community spirit and personal spirituality. It featured workshops from yoga to Aboriginal bushfoods and batik making, group chanting, meditations, dome-building and permaculture. The festival was organised by the Australian Union of Students, and instead of the half a million revellers at Woodstock it attracted only ten thousand punters, yet its impact was long lasting. It was the beginning of the back-to-the-land movement in Australia. Its spirit rescued the village of Nimbin from oblivion. Communes sprouted over hills and valleys. The Northern Rivers became the Rainbow region. The hippie philosophy reached the coast and transformed the ravaged ex-timber logging-sandmining-whaling-abattoir of our town, Byron Bay, making it a sought-after escape for environmentalists, yoga teachers, artisans, musicians, urbanites and, eventually, two million tourists each year. For me the festival meant a reset of my values and a rebirth. My catharsis came with a soundtrack. Few musicians featured at the Aquarius festival; only two were international guests. The Bauls of Bengal, a wild bunch of wandering Bengali minstrels, chanting and ringing their cymbals, high on hash. Dollar Brand was the other one.

South African pianist, Dollar Brand, who later renamed himself Abdullah Ibrahim, was born in Cape Town of mixed-race heritage, classified as coloured under the apartheid regime. Cape Town is where I first set foot on the African continent, but my remembrances are undistinguished. I only disembarked from the ship for a few hours and am left with the memory of an attack of diarrhea resulting from my condition of Crohn's disease, and making my way hastily to a toilet on the first floor of a department store, struggling up the stairs on crutches after breaking my toes on the ship following an unfortunate scuffle with the captain. Some battles in life you win, and some you lose. Dollar must have thought so too, and he left the repressive state in the 1960s for New York and Europe to become one of the world's best known jazz pianists.

Dollar in concert was a marvel to behold and I followed him everywhere, smitten like a teenage girl, adoringly at the front of every stage. His style was an exhilarating, free form fusion of the percussive hammering of the traditional marimba bands of the Cape province, church hymns, the lengthy improvisations of Indian ragas and the modern jazz of Duke Ellington and Thelonious Monk. All this was effortlessly blended in one long stream that ushered you through exuberance, rapture, sorrow, serenity and wonder. The experience was a milestone in my life. Dollar Brand gave me an unforgettable case of *Tarab*, the Arabic notion of ecstasy and reverence that comes from being deeply moved by music or poetry, a consistent driving force in my life. His Aquarian concerts became the leitmotif of my new direction, a return to connect with nature in the land I now called home.

14

KEITH JARRETT

I moved back to Sydney after spending a year with my girlfriend Shanti in a tiny hut on a forested ridge of the Bulga plateau, five hundred metres above the falls of the Ellenborough river. The land had been through a failed hippy community experiment and only my friend Bradley was left in a farmhouse on a hill above the river. On previous walks in the woods I had come upon an abandoned A-framed hut inside the edge of the forest. A Buddhist nun had dwelled there in retreat and Bradley was happy to let us lodge there. No one else would want to. There were no doors or windows and it was a steep hike to get there. I had left the city to recover from a bad episode of Crohn's disease – a sickness I have suffered from since my late teens. 'Rest and tranquillity. No stress!' the doctor prescribed when I left the hospital. This shack, far from the madding world, was the ideal place for a simple existence of daily meditation and contemplation, writing and singing. 'Along the cool sequestered vale of life they kept the noiseless tenor of their way' wrote Thomas Gray. There were no amenities. No power, no radio, recorded music nor fridge. We woke with the first light, slept soon after dark on a rough bed, roofed, but open to the forest, distant from human activities, sheltered in an enchanted world of giant eucalypt trees and rainforested gullies, blending into the natural cycle of things. Water was carried up in buckets from the creek. We shat in a dug trench, built a coop to defend our chickens from goannas, pythons and foxes, milked a cow and made cheese. I sat patiently by mosquito-ridden water pools photographing wildlife, thrice tripping on clean LSD. Shanti and I kept a garden of greens, chopped wood and cooked on an open fire under the stars, gazing into its embers to dream. The year was a gift from the gods.

In our absence the city had moved on. As fashions come and go, I have long realised that you have not really missed anything when you disappear for a time. Much of it is locally based and transient. The latest book, band, film or fad is as relevant to human life as the colour of one's socks. Yet some things had changed. We had landed in a large mansion overlooking a park in Double Bay, in the eastern suburbs of Sydney. An odd mob had settled in this grand but run down residence, set among a genteel and conservative neighbourhood. I believe the governor was a neighbour. A surfer was building a boat in our back garden and raised flags with slogans to annoy the governor. 'DOLLARS IS ALL YOU HAVE!' A German woman downstairs had transformed the once-handsome front yard into a fenced-off mining site, excavated by a pack of Weimaraner hounds that she was breeding to sell. There was a cool bass player from Reunion Island and a heroin addict taking time out. I was doing menial jobs, hoping for better tidings. We had come to work in the city to save up to buy our own patch of wilderness up north with the plan of going back to the land to build a house, plant orchards and gardens, fences and dams. Nature's call had a grip on me.

The fragrance of camelias hung in the air. I was lying on my bed beside the wide open window while the sky turned orange, then a bishop's purple to silken grey, above the darkening park. I closed my eyes and let my mind drift from the shore on the gentle lapping waves of Sibelius' 'Karelia Suite'. When I woke up it was dark. Lindsay walked in with a cup of tea. Lindsay and his girlfriend lodged in the room next to mine on the first floor. He was buoyant.

'Man, you have to come and listen to this new album I bought. I have never heard anything like it.'

His room was twice the size of mine. A built-in wardrobe, a king-sized bed, a fine sound system, a burgundy fleecy woollen carpet up to the edge of a balcony with cane chairs, a table and a view. 'Enjoy!' he said and left me alone with a box set of Keith Jarrett's acoustic piano concerts recorded in Bremen and Lausanne. I dimmed the lights, dropped the needle on side one and stretched out on the carpet where I remained, only to get up to turn over the six sides of three albums. When I had played them all I returned to the start to hear them again. One continuous spell, an adventure of heart and mind, an unclassifiable musical journey that demanded a non-judgemental openness, outside of expectations, narrow definitions, rules and boxes. Keith's fingers tapped a spontaneous composition on the black and white keys, channelling the muses, changing the mood from romantic to exuberant, reflective to exalted. Hints of blues, gospel, boogie, atonal jazz, impressionism, free explorations. The records forged a direct pathway within me to the concerts of Dollar Brand I had witnessed at the Aquarius festival in Nimbin a few years earlier, a major ecstatic experience. It transcended words. In a later interview, I read that Jarrett retorted 'All interviews are bullshit' to a Rolling Stone journalist trying to pin down his process in futile sentences. The discs have become part of my desert island collection. When my youngest brother, Luc, got married I sent him a copy halfway around the world, hoping that he would experience in his marriage, the ecstasy I had felt.

Two weeks later, I left the house. A new job offer had come out of the blue and I had become a co-manager, with Peter, the son of the owner of an exclusive import record shop in the main street of trendy Double Bay. With the job came a spacious apartment, a stroll from the Bay, a stroll from the shop. For a music maniac like myself this was the dream job and I remained there for over a year. Peter and I became good friends, both of us music lovers. Each week we would phone the US and the UK to hear the list of new releases and put in our orders. The albums of Led Zeppelin, Queen, Earth Wind and Fire and Stanley Clarke would be available weeks before their Australian release, and of a superior quality pressing. Fans were waiting at our doorstop for the courier who delivered the platters direct from the airport. This being Double Bay, our clientele was diverse. Doctors and barristers ordered opera and classical music. The rages of the day were jazz-rock, country-rock and disco and I made sure to have some of the great, but hardly known, international music stars. Milton Nascimento, Um Khalsoum, Amalia Rodrigues, Tom Jobim, Ravi Shankar, Olatunji, Indian and Japanese, African and South American music. Peter and I were both in the shop when Keith Jarrett's *Koln Concert* arrived in boxes. I had ordered a lot of copies. It was a gamble, but I need not have worried.

I updated my knowledge, delving into the latest fusions of jazz, rock, funk and R&B. Chick Corea and Return to Forever, Stanley Clarke, Billy Cobham, Weather Report, Miles Davis, Herbie Hancock and the majestic Indian-jazz fusion of the Mahavishnu Orchestra. There was jazz-rock and rock-jazz like Steely Dan, Blood Sweat and Tears, Chicago and The Mothers of Invention, and Latin Rock with Santana. Disco music was its poor cousin, often played by the same ace musicians, since that is where the money was. I did not care much for it, though my costumers did.

Jazz fusion was my brand-new bag. When I had arrived in the Double Bay mansion, the rehearsals of Australia's new fusion band, Crossfire, had drifted across the nearby park, floating above the traffic noise on New South Head Road. Some of its founding members, guitarist Jim Kelly, bass player Greg Lyon, drummer Steve Hopes and saxophonist Tony Buchanan, would become my clients at the shop and, fifteen years later, my music teachers when I studied Contemporary Composition at Southern Cross University. All of them played or recorded with The Hottentot Party, the band I founded with Parissa Bouas. Crossfire went on to great fame culminating in their performances at the Montreux Jazz Festival, entering the annals of Australian jazz history.

But our time in the city was done. We had purchased 500 acres of forested ridges and creeks in an almost uninhabited valley of the Ellenborough and Doyles rivers. Once again the music in vogue and the fashions receded from my radar. I joined a bluegrass trio with two banjo players and learned a whole lot of new tunes on the mandolin. 'Nine Pound Hammer', 'Man of Constant Sorrow', 'Shady Grove', 'Pretty Polly', 'Cripple Creek', 'Darling Corey', 'Mule Skinner Blues', Bill Monroe's instrumentals and John Hartford's steamboat songs.

15
BRAZIL

In a side street, not more than a block away from the Praça da Liberdade, the cultural heart of the Brazilian city of Belo Horizonte, stood a Spanish-inspired night club, unassuming from the outside, but for the blackboard that read: 'LA TABERNA, casa de show, vinos e tapas.'

La Taberna was a prime music venue in the night life of the capital of the state of Minas Gerais, a great place to play. In the space beneath was scribbled in chalk: 'Hoje: Renato Tarsia y Carl Cleves.'

When Renato and I walked into the cheerless entrance foyer with a counter and clothes racks, carried our guitars along a poorly-lit corridor and stepped down a narrow staircase, the inside of the tavern appeared startlingly spacious and enchanting. A permanent air of night lingered, infused with a musty whiff of spilt wine and cigarettes. A raised stage fronted the patrons seated at candle-lit tables and in private alcoves against three walls. On the upper level another three galleries looked out at the stage. The furniture, balustrades and stairs were all made from dark wood. It reminded me of a saloon in one of these mythological American Western films. Without the violence or shootouts, that is. Just our guitars and voices, tapas and red wines.

Waiters busied setting the tables and stacking wine bottles in racks behind the bar while Renato and I ran through our soundcheck. The bartender lit the beeswax altar candles of the iron chandeliers with a burning wick attached to a handle and we retired to the dressing room. Soon we heard a murmur of voices. When the patrons were seated, their orders taken and wines had been served Carlos, the cool soft-spoken owner, dimmed the lights and our show began.

I had arrived from the Atlantic coast only a month before and I had instantly, and unexpectedly, fallen into what soon would become a musical career. On my first weekend in town I had performed as a member of a seven-piece band, two weeks later with Renato and a German guitarist, and now as a duo. Soon I would be a solo performer with my own band, my first outfit since my teenage combo, The Dragons. I had been on a rollercoaster since, a year and a half before, the dream cabin in the woods had been built, the orchards planted, a spring dammed to water the gardens, a child born and then, suddenly, it was all over. I should have seen it coming, but had been too absorbed in the earthly toil and the celestial vision. We could no longer remain so isolated. It was time to move on.

With backpacks and a guitar, my three-year-old son Tashi and I set out across the Pacific, taking our time in the slow lane between welcoming villages and towns with music opportunities, entertaining the French army in Papeete, Club Med guests on the isle of Mourea, distracting the patrons in between strip acts in smoky nightclubs in Vina Del Mar, Chile. A promise of music tempted me to come to Belo

Horizonte, a city that had sprouted the Clube da Esquina, a collective of musicians led by Milton Nascimento, Lo and Marcio Borges with an innovative mix of songs that became, together with Tropicalia, the Bahian gang of songwriters led by Caetano Veloso and Gilberto Gil, the most important musical movement in Brazil. Minas Gerais was a country within a country and had long cherished its own musical agenda, mountain music stewed in folklore, classical music, African slave traditions, church music, marinated with jazz and a little Beatles.

Renato and I finished our second set and sat down for supper when two good-looking girls joined us. Sabrina and Sandra were sisters. I could not make out which one was the most desirable. After my solitary year of travelling and parenting, I had become used to acting the lonesome wanderer. Besides a couple of hints from mothers in laidback villages, suggesting a marriage with their daughters, to help me raise my boy and allow me to join the other men on their daily fishing trips, my contact with women had been solely practical. The gorgeous sisters finally cracked my oyster. Sandra and Sabrina were my initiation in the art of Latin love. Advanced lessons were to follow. But there was more than girls that made this evening at La Taberna memorable. Around midnight, just as we were singing our last songs, a handsome, dreadlocked man, with smooth chocolate-coloured skin walked in with his entourage. He stepped up to the stage and asked whether he could sing a few songs after we finished. It was the up and coming superstar of Brazilian jazz-funk-pop, singer-songwriter Djavan, who had just finished a concert at the Palacio des Artes. Surprisingly, Renato was not interested to stay and left me in anticipation with the girls, and with Djavan.

Son of a white street vendor and black mother named Virginia, who worked as a laundress, Djavan was a promising soccer player in his youth, an all-Brazilian dream, but a change of heart made him leave Maceio, a city of palm trees, mangroves, beaches and emerald seas, to try his luck as a musician in Rio de Janeiro where big things could happen. Starting out as a singer in soap operas and crooning in nightclubs, he recorded two albums that attracted attention. His latest song, 'Faltando um Pedaço' (Missing a Piece) was all over the radio. You could not escape it.

Carlos rushed out to welcome Djavan. He was introduced to some of the musicians and hangers on while the waiters laid out fresh tablecloths and napkins. Everyone ordered late-night food and drinks, a habit that is common among touring performers and probably has brought on many a stomach ulcer. The party was animated, sharing impressions and recollections of the night's concert at the Palacio, letting off steam. I was biding my time, the girls and I eating tapas and flirting. Eventually, a pianist began to play, Djavan went on stage and crooned a whole set of American jazz standards. Perhaps it was his way to relax, or to take a distance from his own songs. Perhaps he was nostalgic of his night club days, but I had expected something else. He was after all, a fantastic songwriter.

It was getting late. The sisters left, but I kept hanging in there, waiting for him to surprise me. But he was on the Real Book roll. Slowly the patrons left. The kitchen closed, the waiters removed the table cloths and stacked the chairs.

The cleaners took possession. Sitting on the pavement outside the closed tavern, waiting for his ride into a new dawn, he sang, on request, the first verses of 'Faltando um Pedaço' to the stars, while the few of us still there laughed. It remained a precious memory. Djavan's rise was swift. His next album would feature Stevie Wonder on mouth organ.

On arrival in Brazil I still performed a traveller's mixture of mellow jazz standards, rousing Leadbelly, blues and country-folk tunes, popular demands, bluegrass and Arabic guitar instrumentals, canciones I learned in Chile and Bolivia, forro folk tunes from our time with the fishermen in Bahia and some originals. But all this time my virgin ears were soaking up new sounds, possibilities and emotions expressed in a language that sings, even when reading a manual. The Latin canciones of ardency, pathos and passion were replaced by the Brazilian sweetness, sensuality and saudade. Inspired, I began to write different songs. I learned to appreciate laments and lullabies, discovered complex harmonies and rhythms. The essence of Brazil is rooted in its music. It belongs to the people. Most Brazilians can conjure up a vast repertoire of popular songs from the contemporary to the rich traditions of the past. Lyrics are known by heart and sung by everyone at parties and in bars. Like Africa or India, Brazil offers culture that promises to keep you surprised and inspired for the rest of your time on earth. It is stupendous! Besides a dazzling array of regional folk and dance styles, forever merging and cannibalising, Brazil has it all: from the classical composer Villa-Lobos to the samba masters past and present, the jazz legends Egberto Gismonti and Hermeto Pascual, to heavy rock bands like Sepultura and some of the finest songwriters and poets on the planet: Tom Jobim, Dorival Caymmi, João Gilberto, Caetano Veloso, Gilberto Gil, Milton Nascimento, Chico Buarque, João Bosco, Djavan. Brazil is a nation that knows that a people without a culture is worthless. No heart. No spice. No soul. Sport may provide great entertainment, but its roots are shallow compared to a song by Tom Jobim, a film of Glauber Rocha, a book by Jorge Amado or a poem by Machado de Assis.

Since no one has a reference to a wanderer's past, the traveller has a clean slate to reinvent him or herself, to recalibrate, making a metamorphosis easier. Likewise, If you choose a life of wandering you must learn to leave your old mold aside, its cumbersome harness of taken-for-granted notions and preconceived ideas you might have assumed to be the universal norm. Store it all in a trunk for later reference and look at the world through different glasses. There is nothing more valuable than the mystery of the unknown. Music and language are double doors.

While music rings the front doorbell, language is the key to its inner sanctum, its heart. When living in Chile, my son and I switched, almost instantly, to basic Spanish, even with each other. In Brazil we spoke Portuguese. First one converses tentatively, then you crack your first joke and, soon, you begin to think and dream in the new language and some of its cultural baggage and codes seep in. You have a rendezvous with another way to think and live, with its own value system, its world view and spiritual practices, the relationship between the sexes, its treatment of children and animals, the approach to work, sense of humor, its secrets and sensibilities, the emotional palette so rich in Latin America. Suddenly the world looks new. Fresh possibilities are revealed. Dormant facets of ourselves blossom.

By acquiring knowledge of how others think and perceive the world we become less certain of the knowledge we think we have. We question and we mutate. We truly transform into a different person when speaking another language. Whereas the English, Germans, Flemish, Australians and others often resort to formulas and platitudes like 'my condolences', 'happy anniversary', 'get well' and 'congratulations', an abundance of emotional eloquence is built into the Portuguese language of Brazil. With a rich vocabulary of tenderness and sweetness it knows how to let your heart speak. No letter, message, text or phone call can be without it. Speak kind words, your heart fills with kindness. Use touching words, if you really want to touch the other.

Belo Horizonte was a happening city during the 1980s. Minas Gerais had begun to blossom after years of stifling military rule. Exhibitions, theatre, dance troupes, festivals, concerts and barzinhos offered a never-ending choice. The generals' grip was loosening and I would bear witness to the change-over to democracy during the seven years my son and I made the city our home base. The people of Minas gave us a generous welcome. Fernando da Motta, a man I proudly call my brother, was responsible for getting me there. Fernando and I were confidants, a man with a big heart. He adopted Tashi and me. We shared his flat in the suburb of São Lucas. He designed my first poster and I would l always search out his opinion when challenged. I learned Portuguese from his comic books and his records. While Tashi was at school, my flame, Alicia, and I made love in Fernando's bed or on his carpet. I even wore his clothes when the limits of my wardrobe became obvious.

Renato Tarsia and the classical composer, Marco Antonio Araujo led me into the musical scene of Minas Gerais. Renato was a Brazilian English teacher who wrote country songs. He had a fine band and lots of work. Renato believed that, as a performer, one should behave like a star, and, since I was in Brazil, I should do the same. But I was just a goldfish who swam with the currents into an unfamiliar aquarium the size of the Mediterranean Sea and should not put on airs. Those first months in town, I would often collect Tashi from kindergarten and together we'd strut along the Avenida Contorno, the tree-lined ring around the inner city, past Savassi and up the hill to Santo Antonio to spend the afternoon jamming with Renato while, my son was entertained by his two children. The Tarsias too, felt like family.

Marco Antonio Araujo was a rising Brazilian star—a longhaired cellist in the symphony orchestra of Minas Gerais who composed music that was a blend of progressive rock and erudite classical. He looked like Jimmy Page and loved Yes, Deep Purple and Pink Floyd. Marco had travelled to London to soak up the 'cultural revolution', spoke some English and booked me for my first gig when I arrived in Belo Horizonte. He also happened to live around the corner from my house and we became friends. When planning my first album Marco offered to score my song 'Darjeeling Winter', enamoured with its classical potential. We established a routine. Twice weekly, during our lunch break, I walked over to his house and we faced each other—one steel string guitar (mine) and one classical guitar (Marco's)- across a coffee table with manuscript paper, throwing ideas around, allotting parts to cellos, violins, violas, flutes and French horns, while his wife Déa, a stunning ballet dancer with the contemporary Grupo Corpo, brought in hot cafezinhos. Marco booked his colleagues from the symphony orchestra for the session and directed. They played through the song twice before putting it all down to one-inch tape. I was an apprentice in awe, a folksinger who had never worked with a classical ensemble before. But it was a thrilling experience and I have kept the score in Marco's handwriting in his memory. Marco Antonio Araujo died two years later from a brain aneurism. He was 36 years old.

Over the years I was fortunate to have some of the finest talent in town in my band. We worked hard at our craft. A band is a brotherhood and I shared a myriad of stages, studios and stories with saxophonists Chico Amaral and Jairo Lara, bass players Marcus Gauguin and Ivan Corrêa, guitarists Affonsinho and Augusto Renno, drummers Mario Castelo, Lincoln Cheib and Julinho Venturino, keyboardist Ricardo Fiuza and violinist Murillo Fonseca. With them I recorded my first two albums that also featured members of the symphony orchestra, the police brass band and the avant garde percussion group UAKTI. I was on a peak and would probably still be there, if not for another unexpected turn of events, that just as it all began, caused me to step out of the frame once more.*

---

*See *Dancing with the Bones*—Carl Cleves (2021)

TWENTY YEARS LATER
In Rio de Janeiro two thousand soldiers and paramilitary police had succeeded in recapturing the favela de Alemão from the drug lords, the traficantes. Heavy weapons were employed. On the screen Parissa and I watched tanks crawl up the narrow streets, crushing the burning barrages while army helicopters flew overhead. It was a war zone. Reporters of the TV stations were embedded with the army, shouting at the camera from the frontlines as doors were bashed in and volleys of machinegun fire ricochetted off the walls. An excited woman in a flak jacket informed us that the border of the state of Minas Gerais was sealed to prevent the 'criminosos' from entering.

But here in the capital of Minas it was a day like any other. Early afternoon, and the sun bathed the city with languor. I turned the TV off and Parissa and I stepped down into the bowels of the five storey edifice Fernando da Motta, had patiently built himself on a sky-scraping bluff at the edge of Belo Horizonte with stupendous views over the sprawling hills of the metropolis, the valleys of towering suburbs, mesmerising at any time of day or night. Fernando had come a long way from his humble flat in São Lucas we used to share. He had steered the imagined into an ingenuously designed castle of glass and concrete with a private cinema, a jumbo collection of quadrinhos (comic strips), and a downstairs studio where Parissa and I had been working on new songs for our next album for the German Stockfisch label. Each Sunday Fernando's band, The Gams, rehearsed here. They had been playing together for years but performances were few so, if you would like to hear them, let me know and I will see what I can do.

It was wonderful to be back in Brazil. I almost had forgotten how loved I was here. I was being celebrated. It was a pleasant surprise. Gigs were coming our way without us even trying. Everything was organised by friends and fans in that special roundabout Brazilian way that gave us no choice but to go with the flow of invitations, shows, concerts and jam sessions. TV Minas came to film us on the balcony of Fernando's house and we sang 'Trem Mineiro', written for such an occasion, aching for this return, my homage to Minas Gerais, against the backdrop of a 250-degree panoramic view of this city of almost six million.

La Taberna still existed but had moved several blocks into the centre of Savassi, a district of bars, restaurants, shops and cultural spaces. Carlos was still the boss and the venue had kept its vibe of wine and music. Parissa and I were booked to play a show there. Life was good and I felt in heaven. Like I had never left the city.

Belo Horizonte had expanded on land and in the sky. Giant shopping malls and viaducts, brand-new highways led into town. The Avenida Prudente de Moraes was hardly recognisable, though my simple adobe house still stood on the steep hill of the rua Mangabeira, seemingly forgotten among high rise buildings. I wanted to peep through the window and into the garden, to see if the banana trees were still there, but the front wall that was built after a gang robbed the house now prevented me. Tashi and I had been away for the weekend with the band and, fortunately, I had my guitar and amplifier with me. When we returned we found the house wide open, the door bashed in. 'They must have used an elephant' I thought to myself. Pillows and mattresses had been slashed. The place was stripped. All our belongings were gone. From camera to children's books. We were left with the clothes we had on. Our house bordered a favela and when I complained to the washer-woman that my son had no toys nor clothes left, a garbage bag appeared at my front door with a few T-shirts and shorts -nothing of value, but a gesture nevertheless.

My past collaborators were all musical royalty, often addressed as 'mestre' in that Brazilian way of showing respect to older artists. Eternal matinee idol and hot shot guitarist, Affonsinho, who drank from the fountain of youth, had become an MPB (Musica Popular Brasileira) star with smooth bossa-pop songs with a dash of blues. Lincoln Cheib was now the musical director and drummer for the song king of Minas, Milton Nascimento. Augusto Renno tracked the jazz-rock footprints of Al Dimeola, Pat Metheny and Toninho Horta, while our bearded bear on bass guitar, Ivan Corrêa, flew around Brazil as the musical director for a well-known Sertaneja band and regularly spotlighted in photographs with the pantheon of musical giants of the nation. The erudite instrumental group, UAKTI, went on to tour with Philip Glass and could be heard on Paul Simon's album *Rhythms of the Saints*.

Whiz kid, Gauguin, had chased a different dream. He, who could sing every vocal—lead or harmony—by John, Paul, George or Ringo, play every guitar, bass or piano part of every Beatle song –but not all at once– instructed three others and took his band to Liverpool to become *The Best Beatle Band in the Whole World* against groups from Sweden, Kazakhstan, the USA and everywhere in between. Sergeant Pepper (name of the band) recorded an album of songs The Beatles had written, but never bothered to record themselves -all done in vintage Beatle style- at Abbey road studios.

Saxophonist and composer, Chico Amaral's pop songs had sold millions of discs for another band from Minas, the ska-reggae outfit, Skank. He wrote a biography of Milton Nascimento and now played his hot Latin jazz around town. Parissa and I spent a weekend at his 'sitio', his country hideout, being entertained by Chico singing his infinite repertoire of sambas de raiz, xote, baiâo, forró, American standards and bawdy tunes. Parissa had been jamming with his band, with Fernando da Motta's's rock band, The Gams, with bossa nova and MPB singers Affonsinho and Leri. Parissa's voice was making waves and she was already considered one of the finest singers in town. I am honoured to have created music with these brilliant guys and dear friends. Check out their music.

Parissa and I had boarded an overcrowded bus of sweating bodies into downtown Belo Horizonte to attend a free afternoon concert to celebrate the 62nd anniversary of the Universal Declaration of Human Rights. It was a tropical Sunday, heavy clouds above us, moisture in the air. Crowds were streaming into the Praça da Estação from all directions. A sea of short dresses, jeans, T-shirts and football shorts, sunglasses and chinelas (thongs). Some carried small backpacks with raincoats and bottled water, others nothing but for some coins in a pocket or bra. Everyone was in a jubilant mood, finding a place somewhere near the stage, buying ice creams, lemonade, pasteis and hot dogs from stores and vendors. The military police, armed and wrapped in flak jackets, were ready, but not needed.

Antonio Nóbrega whirled upon the stage in a flare of white cotton pants, a long-sleeved white shirt, a black vest, rimmed with purple, blue, dark green and orange. A roar went up. He tipped a black felt hat, bowed to the crowd, jumped in to the air, tumbled, then lifted his violin to his shoulder and played a breakneck north-eastern tune while dancing the frevo, his body spinning and turning, arcing and arching, never missing a beat, never missing a note. His elegance masked the sheer power and flexibility required.

Frevo is the carnival music of his home town, Recife, the first slave port in the Americas and the capital of the north-eastern state of Pernambuco. Antonio is a cultural icon of his state. Frevo is an acrobatic dance sprung from capoeira, the martial arts of simulated fights, dancers twirling and kicking at each other, with ever more daring and demanding moves, without ever hitting the opponent. Capoeira has spread far beyond its borders.

Antonio Nóbrega was the day's event's dazzling master of ceremonies, part dancer, ace-fiddler, singer and actor, part clown and vagabond, entertaining us with summersaults and miming postures while swinging and swirling a rainbow-coloured umbrella as if it was just another limb of his body, then weaving pirouettes around the desfile of music stars as they entered the stage.

First of the rank was the dame of samba, Elza Soares. She had just turned eighty.

Born in 1930 in a favela in Rio de Janeiro, forced into marriage by her father at twelve and with her first child born within a year, life was not an easy ride. Yet her passion for singing endured and braced her. As many have learned, music is the comfort when you are weeping, the buoy when you are drowning, the hand when you are falling, the balm when your heart is bleeding, the anti-dote from the bite of a viper. If Elza's childhood was tough, her adult life reads like a Greek tragedy. At twenty-one she was a widow, raising five children on her own. Ten years later the Brazilian press, and many in her public, vilified her when she had a love affair with the famous right wing soccer player Garrincha. She was called a witch and a marriage breaker, received death threats. They did marry, but Garrincha had a bad drinking problem. Drunk, he smashed the car, leaving everyone inside wounded. Elza's mother, Dona Rosario, was thrown from the car and killed. Once the greatest dribbler in the nation who led his country to win the World Cup in 1962 when Pele was injured, he had since been on a path of self-destruction in full view of the nation. It was a harrowing sight. Elza went from bar to bar trying to convince barkeepers to stop serving alcohol to her husband, until he died of cirrhosis of the liver. When her nine year old son was killed in a car accident she almost ended her own life but, devastated and deeply depressed, she kept on singing. And here she stood before us. The Great Dame of Samba. Everyone, young and old, knew her successes and sang with her. Elza received an ovation.

The show honoured the songs, and the voice of Minas Gerais, Milton Nascimento, who for more than thirty years had sung his messages of wisdom in a chocolate baritone and lifted our souls with a soaring falsetto, pure as the waterfalls of these mountains, as he chronicled the abuse of the native Indians and the environment, the deep-rooted racism and the harsh existence of rural women. His songs had become anthems of this traditional Brazilian state, the size of France with a population of almost twenty million. When in 1985 Tancredo Neves, the ex-governor of Minas, was elected the first democratic president of Brazil, Milton had sung at the immense rally for democracy on the Avenida Afonso Pena in the heart of the city. For seven years, his songs had been my soundtrack, hearing them daily—in bars, on the radio and at parties. Everyone could sing them.

The forró queen of Paraíba, Elba Ramalho, was followed by another Paraíba superstar, the impish songwriter with a wicked gleam in his eyes and quirky songs, Chico César. As thousands of voices chanted with him

'Mama Africa, a minha mae, é mae solteira.'*

the skies burst open and a mass of people danced in a tropical downpour, soaked to the skin, waving hands above our heads. Nothing could dampen our spirits.

Luiz Melodia grew up in a slum in Rio de Janeiro on one of the morros (steep hills) poking out above the Bay of Guanaraba. A cool black dude who had acquired an aura of Rimbaud, le poète maudit, with his mixture of samba, a little blues, a little rock and soul. He lived a wild life, but his

---

*Mother Africa, my mother, is a single mum.

album *Perola Negra* (Black Pearl) remained an all-time classic. Parissa and I went looking for a snack and returned as Luiz left the stage with Antonio Nóbrega dancing circles around him while Lenine came on. I am a fan. His album *Olho de Peixe*, recorded with percussionist Suzano is a milestone, forever stored in the safe of my desert island collection. 'Relampiano', his haunting song about a child street vendor on the streets of a metropolis, is Brazil's own 'Strange Fruit'. There was a commotion on the side of the stage and then it happened. Lenine was joined by Milton Nascimento himself to sing 'Paciência', a heartbreaking ballad that gave one goose bumps. I was in tears and realised I had felt like an orphan during all those years of my absence.

> O mundo vai girando
> Cada vez mais veloz
> A gente espera do mundo
> E o mundo espera de nós
> Um pouco mais de paciência
> (Dudu Falcão / Lenine)

> The world keeps turning
> Faster each time
> We all ask the world
> And the world asks us
> A little more patience

The following day it was still bucketing rain, the car slipping and sliding up the muddy mountain track towards Lavras Novas, a village high on a hilltop beyond the old capital of

Minas, Ouro Preto. Lavras was founded by gold diggers in the early 1700's after the seams of Ouro Preto were exhausted. My friends Claudinha and Carlos drove Parissa and me through the cobble-stoned streets past brightly coloured one-storey houses, shouting greetings to people sitting on their doorstep watching the rain, past the old church of Nossa Senhora dos Prazeres (Our Lady of the Pleasures) to the pousada, the small hotel our friends had built on the outskirts of the village overlooking the mountain ranges, where we would be playing that night.

Several of my heroes had passed through the capital over recent weeks: João Bosco, Lenine and Egberto Gismonti who gave me a case of *tarab*—tears, goose bumps et al. And so, we decided to soak it up and linger in Minas until the new year began a fresh breeze.

16
WORLD MUSIC

hen I first came to Australia I was branded a Belgian; when I lived in Brazil the Mineiros typecast me as an Australian; and when I returned to Australia in 1988, everyone called me a Brazilian. I guess I have a foot in all these camps. 'Roots are not in landscape or a country, or a people, they are inside you,' wrote Isabel Allende. Nationality has never meant that much to me -people do. Humanity's football club mentality is so often abused by politicians: our team is better than your team. Rally round the flag. Flags are used for wrapping lies or strengthening the authority of the leaders. For God, king and country are outdated concepts. It's a short walk from patriotism to fascism.

Well, here I was again, a true blue Aussie, disguised as a Brazilian. I had not lived in Sydney for twelve years and most of my old music buddies had either left town or succumbed to drink or religion, after round-the-clock gigs in pubs. I explored the nightlife now and then, in search of music and friends. The scene had metamorphosed from butterfly to blowfly. Hippies were out. It was all punk, funk and be hip in the late eighties. Bands were too cool to fool; no one smiled; punters, dressed in black, danced without touching. I stepped into the Evil Star and the Annandale Hotel wearing my batik Brazilian shirt and white pants, and everyone treated me like I was an undercover cop. A decade of local pop music had passed me by. While my ears had been soaking up Caetano Veloso, João Bosco, Gilberto Gil, Milton Nascimento, Egberto Gismonti, Luiz Gonzaga and Pixinguinha, I had missed out on The Cure, Duran Duran, Depeche Mode, Billy Idol, Kylie Minogue, Adam and the Ants, Wham, George Michael and so much more Anglo-American jingle jangle that had dominated the Australian airwaves. I was out of touch. A stranger in a strange land again.

Even the city landscape had mutated. A grand new complex had risen at Darling Harbour. Sydney had become more self-assured. The Labour Party was in power and the nation seemed positive, though some years later John Howard, a barnacle stuck to the hull of the good ship Charlotte that had arrived with the First Fleet to offload the empire's cargo of unwanted convicts, would take over to become the deputy sheriff of George W. Bush, enlist Australia in another US invasion and history would repeat itself. But for now, the Bicentennial celebrations sprouted exhibitions and cultural events around town. There were more Asians on the streets, more Thai and Vietnamese restaurants on the block. How the Australian palate had come of age since the days of pork chops, baked beans and vegemite. Italians and Greeks had seen to that, followed by the Chinese, Lebanese, Turkish and South East Asians cuisines. Multi-culturalism was the buzz-word, and I liked it. I joined The Voices from the Vacant Lot, a choir that wore extravagant hats and sang songs from Bulgaria, Senegal, Guadaloupe, South Africa, Nicaragua and 16TH century Spain. There were eighteen of us. When we went on mini-tours to festivals, to Canberra or the Blue Mountains, it became a tribal affair with partners and children tagging along. I began to make friends, establish heart connections. Home is where the heart is.

Meanwhile the recording industry had gone through a conversion, in search of novelty. In an attempt to escape the sameness of the tired Anglo-saxon rock and pop formulas, the music from other cultures suddenly became more readily available. Small labels such as Shanachie, Harmonia Mundi, Smithsonian Folkways, Sterns, World Circuit and others provided rare music from distant corners. English pop star Peter Gabriel founded Real World Records and the Womad festivals, giving us the chance to see foreign music legends live and purchase their records. Qawwali star from Pakistan, Nusrat Fateh Ali Khan, the Congolese king of rumba-rock and soukous Papa Wemba, Tibetan diva Yunchen Lhamo, and unknown gems like Ayub Ogada and Geoffrey Oryema from East Africa, Farafina from Burkina Faso and Värttinä from Finland received international acclaim. An avalanche of new musical ideas offered themselves. For someone who had grown up with the music library of my home town of Mechelen and wandered for years through Africa, Asia, the Pacific islands and Latin America in search of musical bliss, this all made sense. My brother Luc had sent me cassette tapes when I lived in Brazil where these recordings were still inaccessible.

The day Parissa Bouas and I met we sang through a gamut of music, from bossa nova and blues, Andean music and salsa, to South African trade union and popular songs. Rarely did I meet someone who enjoyed such a broad spectrum. I had recently arrived from Brazil and she from Central America, where she had gone coffee-picking with the international brigade in support of the Sandinista revolution, but ended up joining a travelling Andean music ensemble. Soon we were busking together on the streets of Sydney and became lovers. When enrolled in a Contemporary Music course at Southern Cross University (SCU), in Lismore, 750 kilometres north of Sydney, we were ready for a creative explosion. We called ourselves The Hottentots, with a repertoire from Persia, Egypt, Martinique, Africa, Latin America, children's tunes and world pop and had landed on fertile ground at SCU. It was a bountiful time. Experienced musicians with a track record crossed with hugely talented young ones, direct from high school, spawning original bands of various genres, like mushrooms sprouting in cow pats after a summer downpour.

The Hottentots extended into The Hottentot Party, with an intention to explore and fuse this new treasure grove of musical possibilities. The world was our oyster. We played a spicy dance stew of originals, ska, reggae, mbaqanga, mixed Argentinian chacarera with Indian tabla talk, the two female singers, Rochelle and Parissa, experimented with Bulgarian throat singing and creative yodelling. We flirted with time signatures, African guitar styles and innovative grooves, flavoured fun with funk.

One sultry north coast night, sweating over an assignment on swing band music, a Caribbean dance floor hit burst from the university Radio Station 2NCR. The song was 'Rete' by a Paris-based band from Guadaloupe, Kassav, who had modernized a Caribbean carnival music named compas, a modern merengue that Haitians had been dancing to since the 1800s, and renamed it zouk. I instantly forgot all about swing bands and had written a chorus and some verses before 'Rete' had faded from the airwaves. 'A Long Way' was the first song the band recorded and it won the NCEIA (North Coast Entertainment Industry Association) Award for Best World music. It became the opening track of our first album, *A Small World*, that went on to win the Album of the Year Award (1994) and resulted in a string of high profile gigs at major festivals around Australia. *A Small World* was a flash of lightning. There was so much energy in that CD that the plastic case vibrated. A gumbo stew of rhythms from Africa, Brazil, the Caribbean and Bulgaria with dollops of funk, blues, poetry, pop and politics. And everyone danced. The album, and the five ones that followed, were monumental milestones in the soundtrack of my life over the coming years.

The original Hottentot Party: Nicolette Boaz, Parissa Bouas, Carl Cleves, Kath Davis, Rik Cole

17

THE QUEEN OF MALAGASY MUSIC

A LAND OF MYSTERY AND MYTH

Madagascar is a land of mystery and myth. Its plants and animals, people and landscape are a strange puzzle. The fourth largest island in the world drifted away from the African continent 160 million years ago and, during this long isolation, its flora and fauna developed independently from the rest of the world, with the result that 80% of all its animals and vegetation are unique to the island.'

I paused, pressed a key on the laptop. Two ring-tailed lemurs appeared on the large screen above my head. And so, another two-hour class had commenced in Y Block, the large auditorium of Southern Cross University in Lismore, where I was lecturing in World Music. Each Thursday morning, at nine o'clock, the eighty-four students and I put on our fabulous travelling shoes to dash off to Ireland or Cuba, hang out on the banks of the Niger river or in the bazaars of Cairo. We might fancy a vodka at a rowdy Bulgarian wedding; sweat and sway a sexy samba to a boisterous batucada in Rio; scrape the washboard and rattle the spoons at a zydeco hoedown in the Louisiana swamplands;

or eavesdrop in a Mumbai Bollywood recording studio, where elderly female playback singers croon like teenage sparrows. Was there a better way to spend a morning in Lismore? I enjoyed myself, and hoped that I could panpipe my students down the magical musical rabbit hole with me. On the screen above me giant water-gorged baobabs and tiny chameleons paraded, forbidding landscapes of thirty metres high limestone needles, forests of tentacled thorn trees, while the music of Madagascar's most famous export, the band Tarika, bounced through the speakers.

'Madagascar was the last place on earth to be populated by humans,' I continued, 'the first inhabitants only arrived around 300 AD. They were of Malayo-Polynesian origin. How they got there is a mystery, but the Malagasy language can be traced to areas that are now situated in Malaysia and Indonesia. The features of some of the Malagasy tribes, especially the Merina and Betsileo, are distinctly Asian.'

Magnified on the screen, Hanitra Rasoanaivo's dark eyes looked down at the students, her shiny black hair cut short, trimmed around the ears. Her milk chocolate-and-cinnamon Sulawesi skin glowed. What a stunning woman! Sensual lips, a turquoise stud in her ear, a turquoise-studded necklace round a slender neck and, draped over her right shoulder, a woven lamba of rich Indian red and purple stripes. Hanitra stared out defiantly from the cover of Tarika's most successful album, *Son Egal*, against a golden background featuring photos of a Senegalese woman and of the last queen of Madagascar, Queen Ranavalona III, taken in the 1890s when she was sent into exile in Algeria by the French colonisers, who declared French the official language and abolished the Merina monarchy. The French had followed the English. The English had followed the Portuguese. Marco Polo might have been the first white man to report on the great red island, but before that, Arab traders and settlers from the East African coast had already been added to the mix. Pirates too, had found a safe haven in its forested and sheltered bays, from where they raided the ships of the East India Company. Daniel Defoe claimed that a French pirate with a Robin Hood bent, named Misson, had established a utopian republic on the north coast of the island, with its own parliament, printing press and international language. Fact or fiction? Madagascar is indeed a land of puzzles and mystery.

When I first heard the musical traditions of this island I was astounded. I couldn't figure out the connections. One piece sounded Asian, another African. When I played examples to my students, one ventured that it was Mexican, another thought it was a late Renaissance European composition. There were furious rhythms and melancholic songs, bizarre string instruments, flutes and drums, rich Polynesian harmonies, percussive breathing that seemed from another era, another world. Years earlier I had seen my first Malagasy band live. It was during a mini-festival in the city of Brisbane. The Justin Vali trio performed on a bill with the South African mbaqanga stars, the groaning Mahlathini and the jiving Mahotella Queens, and the Malian singer with the albino face and the golden voice, Salif Keita.

Justin Vali was a virtuoso performer of the valiha, a tubular zither made from bamboo, the national instrument, brought by his ancestors from the island of Borneo. Its twenty-one strings are delicately plucked with the fingers of both hands like a harp. Angels in heaven play the valiha when God takes his siesta. Justin was accompanied by a frizzy-haired man who strummed a peculiar square-boxed guitar with partial frets, the kabosy, while another dazzling guitarist picked out quirky bass lines, quite independent of the higher melody notes played on the valiha. His name was Doudou, and I talked to him after the show about his unusual guitar tunings. I was hooked and began researching the music of Madagascar seriously, tracking down every book or recording I could find.

A week before the year 2000 Parissa and I were invited by the Woodford Folk Festival to compose an anthem for the new millennium—to be performed and televised at the midnight hour.

'I need a rousing piece in waltz time of exactly six minutes long,' requested Neil Cameron, the wizard director of the festival's grand Fire Event.

We found our inspiration in the music of Madagascar. Using one of Justin Vali's songs 'Rambala' as a foundation,

THE QUEEN OF MALAGASY MUSIC

Parissa and I set to work with piano and guitar. Within a day or two we had added new sections to the tune and written the words to 'Put your Hand in Mine'. Giant effigies went up in flames, throwing searing cinders into the midnight sky when a seven hundred-piece choir, conducted by Parissa, initiated the new millennium before a multitude of thousands, chanting on the grassy hills. Let go of the old! Embrace the future as one! The six minutes of 'Put your Hand in Mine' were simultaneously transmitted by satellite to 1.6 billion people in sixty countries around the world. It was shown on a giant screen on Time Square and on every continent. But Madagascar was not among those countries. One of the poorest nations in the world, it seemed that this intriguing island had somehow fallen off the map. Rarely visited by tourists before the nineteen-nineties, four hundred kilometres off the African coast in the vast Indian Ocean, Madagascar was not on the way to anywhere, and was never in the news. But its music had a hold on me.

ANTANANARIVO, THE CAPITAL OF MADAGASCAR

We disembarked at Ivato airport in the middle of the night, made our way through the gates and were instantly tackled by a swarm of pestering porters. Hands clawed at our suitcases, pulled our guitars in different directions and held on to Parissa's handbag.

'Monsieur! Viens avec moi.'

'Hotel, madame, très bien!'

'Taxi, par ici monsieur!'

We were the only foreigners on the flight, lambs thrown into a melee of ravenous wolves. I struggled to keep hold of my guitar case.

'Antshow! Antshow! Par ici.'

A young man grabbed me by the arm and shouted at the porters in a melodic but incomprehensible tongue. We followed him to a ramshackle Citroen Deux Chevaux, piled our instruments and suitcases into the tiny car and sped off into night. Sandy was our chauffeur. He was the bass player of *Tarika Be*, Hanitra Rasoanaivo's latest outfit, and her younger brother. On this first night we were just too exhausted to take it in, peering out of the windows while Sandy drove us through the dark labyrinth of narrow and rutted streets, straining up the hills of this vast and, at this hour, deserted city of Antananarivo. We arrived at an imposing building, towering above the surrounding houses and shacks. Sandy banged on an immense iron gate until a night watchman appeared. Both men helped us upstairs with our luggage into a comfortable clean room with a double bed and two night tables fashioned of cane and lacquered green. On the bed lay two white towels and bathrobes with the silhouette of Hanitra's features embroidered on them. I couldn't believe we had made it here.

For years I had been trying to find a connection to the musical world of Madagascar. Several promising leads had fizzled out. My friend, percussionist Blair Greenberg, had met a woman who knew everyone in the Malagasy music scene, only to lose her phone number. The music itself was hard to find. There were few CDs -and these were released on obscure independent labels. But the Law of Attraction, that has sold many millions of self-help books, also worked for me, and so it happened that Ian Anderson, editor of Folkroots, the English world music magazine, finally brought me into contact with Hanitra. I had downloaded and photocopied Ian's articles about the music of Madagascar; read them so often that I had memorised the names of the musicians and places where he had travelled. I began corresponding with Hanitra and sent her our CDs. She invited us to come and stay at the cultural centre she had built in Tana, which is what the locals call their city, Antananarivo.

Antshow is a grand, three-storey complex with guest rooms, a studio and concert space with a bar, a dining room and a hairdressing salon. Hanitra herself lives on the top floor. She and her dynamic father had designed the huge edifice in the red brick Merina style, intending to promote the local arts and provide a space for concerts, exhibitions, rehearsals, workshops and press conferences, a place where artists could meet and collaborate. It was an ambitious plan. Somehow, they had succeeded in building this enormous place in the middle of a revolution, while the country was at a virtual standstill, petrol and electricity scarce, and with all building supplies needing to be carried in manually. Hanitra is a visionary powerhouse.

Parissa and I were looking at the pictures of African superstars displayed on the walls of the dining room—Oumou Sangare, Sally Nyolo, Youssou Ndour—usually in the company of Hanitra – when a shy girl brought in a plate with paw paw slices. Crispy French loaves, a small dish with butter and a pot of coffee stood on a white napkin. Hanitra strode in. A floppy grey jumper hung over black tights. The hair above her ears was shaved in a straight line from front to back. Even fresh out of bed, she was more attractive than in her promo photos.

'Welcome to Antshow.'

She pecked us on both cheeks. I introduced ourselves in French and we handed her the gifts we had brought from Australia: chocolate-coated macadamia nuts, indigenous artefacts and the large box of second-hand guitar strings I had collected from my students at university.

'Thank you very much. My apologies, but I 'd rather speak English than French.'

She poured coffee and we sat down to breakfast.

'In Madagascar my name is actually pronounced as Anch' she said—a bit of a disappointment as I had rather liked the sound of Hanitra.

But we soon learned that the pronunciation of words in this complex multi-syllabic language varied greatly from the written form. Multi-syllabic is an understatement too, considering the 18th century Madagascan king who went by the name of Andrianampoinimerinandriantsimitoviaminandriampanjaka. Most of the Malagasy words we had memorised, by pasting them on to our bathroom walls back home, sounded totally different from the way we had practiced them. Vowels and syllables vanished; stresses were not where you might expect. Misotra, or thank you, became misotr; manao ahoana, or hello, became amanaona; vazaha or foreigner was pronounced as vaza. Tarika turned into Tark and Hanitra into Anch. Antshow was really Hanitra's show. She enunciated the words slowly, her dark eyes on Parissa who repeated them and took notes. We all laughed. Hanitra's enthusiasm was contagious. Buoyant and jovial, she radiated charisma and charm. An aura of twinkles surrounded her. After a flurry of conversation over coffee and baguettes, a tradition that the Malagasy have inherited from the French, Hanitra advised us to get a feel of the capital, 'dip a toe in the lake.' (I speak metaphorically, and do not advise anyone to dip body parts into Lac Anosy in Antananarivo.)

'Explore' she said, and left us to our own devices.

It was the beginning of August, the middle of winter, cold and windy in the central highlands. A feeble sun broke through the pollution as Parissa and I boarded a minibus to the city centre, some six kilometres from Antshow. The transport system of Madagascar is less comfortable but more efficient than the one I was used to in Sydney, where one might need over an hour and three buses to reach the beach from a suburb only a few kilometres away. In Tana a minibus passes every five or ten minutes. No seat is wasted. I counted twenty-eight people in our tiny bus, with passengers passing their children around to sit on other people's laps. The ticket money was handed down from person to person to the collector who was swinging halfway out of the vehicle. It was not unusual to share three seats with seven commuters. At most stops we all disembarked and re-embarked to let other travellers out. Our first outing to Tana was a shock, but we soon became accustomed to being once again in a struggling third world city with potholed streets, congested traffic, decrepit cars blowing clouds of blue diesel. Before starting a journey, taxi drivers bought fuel in plastic containers and switched off their motors when rolling downhill.

Tana is a city of hills and valleys and, like the island itself, the capital is a puzzle: houses cling to hillsides that could have been somewhere in the Andes; middle class suburbs are reminiscent of small European towns; overcrowded ghettos -like those found in large African cities- mushroom. And then, beneath the built-up hills lay valleys and marshes, with terraced rice fields and green gardens that could have been lifted from rural Indonesia or Vietnam. Like most third world cities Tana had burgeoned, almost overnight, into a city of three million inhabitants. There was a constant need for more housing. The main building materials of Merina architecture are clay for the walls and tin, or thatch, for the roofs. Scattered among Tana's hills lay valleys, dug up by brick makers who mined the red topsoil for clay and fired the stacked bricks in kilns on site. The merry chatter of children gushed from a haze of smoke.

On this first morning, Parissa and I wandered around the lower town, stalked by peddlers hawking cars made from tin cans, toy lemurs, poorly made valihas and ornaments carved from zebu horn. We climbed up steep staircases and along narrow streets into the Haute Ville, where we quickly got lost. Street signs are rare in Tana. Few people still spoke the colonial French. The French, after all, had left almost fifty years earlier. But losing ourselves, on this first day, in this intriguing city was just fine. Parissa chirped. I gesticulated like Alice down the rabbit-hole. Tentatively, we practiced our local greetings and bought fruit and baguettes at the teeming Analakely markets, struggling with the varied dirty banknotes of different sizes. Two currencies were active side by side: the old-style Malagasy franc and the new ariary. Even the marketeers needed digital calculators.

The Deux Chevaux taxi driver who drove us up to the Rova Palace made us pay in advance, then bought petrol. The car strained and struggled, backfiring all the way up. Wires were hanging from the dashboard like a gutted animal and the driver kept steering with his head out the window anxiously looking at his rear wheel, while narrowly avoiding oncoming traffic. I feared that the wheel was about to come off. A trail of blue smoke and red dust followed in our wake. The Rova Palace stood on the highest hill of the city. From up here, the psychopathic queen Ranavalona I had ordered the Christians to be thrown from the cliffs. This feared 19th century Merina ruler was a nymphomaniac with a sadistic streak, constantly devising new ways to torture her perceived enemies. Prisoners were sawn in half or drenched in boiling water, sewn up in sacks and left to slowly perish, or to be amputated limb by limb. Thankfully she was long gone. Her palace had been destroyed in a fire in 1995. It was closed for repairs. Flocks of crows whirled around the towers, straight out of the scene of Mordor in *Lord of the Rings*.

I was instantly charmed by the Malagasy people. It was easy to like their amiable, polite and calm manner. It prevailed in the crowded buses, on the streets, in markets, shops, stalls and restaurants. The discreet charm of the Malagasy was very different from the exuberance and pushiness I had become used to in African or Asian cities. Even the beggars here responded with a smile or greeting, when we had run out of coins and there was nothing left to give.

Throughout all our travels on the red island my impression never changed. I felt safe and at ease. A greeting in Malagasy always evoked a jovial response. The Malagasy were extraordinarily patient and resilient, even in the most trying of circumstances. In contrast with the ferocious battles to board an Indian railway carriage, in Madagascar there were no queue jumpers. When travelling long distances in uncomfortable, ridiculously overloaded taxi brousse vehicles that were prone to breakdowns, no one complained - even children didn't whimper. Parents everywhere doted on their offspring, especially the fathers. The macho behaviour I had encountered elsewhere is toned down in Madagascar, tempered by gentleness, manners and reserve.

MERINA MUSIC

The Piment café was a nasty, almost empty, little dive near a dirty lake buzzing with mosquitoes. Hanitra and Njaka -her companion in the band- had brought us here to hear Kalibera, the star wizard of the Merina guitar players. I went into rapture, regardless of the pervading stink of the overflowing toilet. By the time we left, the hive was pumping. It was our first night out in Madagascar and it heralded many experiences of enchantment and bliss in the sacred temples of sound, hovels of rhythm and song. To top it off, in the car on the way home, Hanitra invited us to do a show with her in three weeks time.

We settled into a routine: Parissa and I practiced daily with Hanitra, her multi-instrumentalist Njaka and guitarist Solo, and explored the city in our free time. The rehearsals were exciting. Just to hear Hanitra sing and Njaka play his marovany, valiha or kabosy was a thrill.

'The concert will be a marriage of Hottentot and Tarika,' she announced, 'a musical handshake between two islands separated by the Indian Ocean.'

Parissa and I would learn their songs, while they attempted to play ours. This was more exacting than it sounds. The Malagasy language isn't easy; the syncopation of the music a challenge. For them too our songs, with their blues feels and odd time signatures, were a test. Traditional Malagasy string instruments are diatonic and played in one key, so that modulation is impossible without changing or retuning instruments. The rubbing of cultures created sparks.

But there was another stumbling block. I had been robbed of my voice, straining my vocal chords when writing a new song in a high register. I had visited a voice clinic in Brisbane ten days before travelling and was ordered to keep silent for six weeks. Parissa did not speak French. She had to rely on me to ask for directions, buy food and communicate. My wife was taking a crash course in Malagasy. Although she has a knack with languages and easily parrots the melodic contour and tongue-twisters of foreign speech, progress was slow. I tried to talk as little as possible, communicating with pen and paper, while dripping manuka honey down my throat every few hours, gargling with warm salty water and steaming with eucalyptus oil. It would be a while nonetheless before I returned to my previous Caruso condition. It was ironic that, after dreaming for years about this moment, that now that I was going to perform with one of my favourite bands, I had no voice. And so I strummed my guitar, while Parissa had to sing all the Malagasy lyrics of Tarika's songs, as well as my songs in awkward keys. She is a trooper.

Hanitra was raised in the forest, but that area is close to where Antshow is built now, and the forest of her childhood has been swallowed up by the voracious capital. Her mother and father, who still lived nearby, always sang together with their four children. Both her sister Noro and her brother Sandy were members of Tarika Be, the most recent incarnation of the band. Occasionally the family still performed together. Her father often dropped by at Antshow in the morning. He was a feisty, seventy-five year-old, thrilled by my love for the music of Madagascar. He spoke little French. Hanitra translated. When I mentioned that I was searching for the old time Merina music named

Kalon 'Ny Fahiny, he beamed with excitement and pride. This old-time music from the 1920s and 30s was his favourite music. The Merina were his people. He instantly broke into a song. He recommended a run-down theatre in a rather scruffy part of town, where one could still hear this slowly vanishing tradition each Sunday afternoon. We went to check it out.

The municipal theatre in Isotry sat in a poor neighbourhood, the pavements crowded with hawkers selling vegetables, fruit and lambas –the Malagasy sarongs. Across the street from the theatre stood a white and red painted house selling the local Three Horses beer. Laundry was drying on all the iron railings that framed the first floor verandahs of the traditional Merina houses. A now familiar rancid Tana smell hung in the air. We were the first to arrive. Tickets were cheap.

Slowly a small audience drifted in, mostly dignified old people and parents with children, dressed in their Sunday best, the gentlemen in striped suits, the ladies with white shawls draped over their shoulders. People eyed us with interest. What were these vazaha doing here? A choir of a dozen singers, young and old, small and tall, walked onto the stage to deliver two rousing songs. Then the faded, grey velvet curtain swung open and the theatrical performance commenced. Though it all took place in Malagasy, it was not difficult to follow this Romeo and Juliette romance. A quaint operetta of bygone days, here called vakindazana, unfolded in which actors regularly burst into song in the middle of a conversation while, now and then, two singers interrupted the intrigue to comment on the plot with stately

Kalon-style renditions, accompanied by a piano player in a fashion seemingly borrowed from the traditional valiha. It was a tame affair. There were no flights of tarab to be had in Isotry on that day and we left the theatre at the interval to eat a tough zebu steak in a nearby 'hotely', as the small informal restaurants serving basic meals are called.

Now that daddy Rasoanaivo knew of our interest he accompanied us to a rural crafts fair and, on his advice, we checked out a musical event on the northern edge of town. In the burning sun we lounged on the grass all day, amongst a large Malagasy crowd, to listen to a bewildering variety of performers. The all-day festival was sown together by the imposing orations of Ramilison, the veteran champion-master of kabary, the poetic art of public speech. He was dressed in an impeccable suit with a broad-brimmed hat and seemed strangely Mexican.

High energy bands from the south sped through their tsapika and mangaliba tunes, riffing on their square guitars, the kabosy, urging on their star dancers to light a fire. But in the heat of the day, the audience was too lethargic to dance. Only Parissa was shaking her hips. Even in her sleep her legs jerk to the tunes in her dreams. Pretty young girls took to the stage to croon the revolting syrupy 'poopy pop' songs that were the rage among teenagers. Luke-warm evangelical Christian groups tried, and failed, to rouse the crowd to conversion, but a Malagasy country and western outfit in black cowboy hats and golden-tassled blue shirts had more success. This band's harmonies sounded more like Thursday Island than Nashville, but the mini-skirted, frenetic, black dancing girls were pure Malgash.

Then there were majestic performances of Hiragasy troupes of singers, musicians and costumed dancers, the men in red coats and straw hats and the women in long, colorful dresses. Hiragasy is the quintessential Merina cultural expression, a veritable bardic art, a play of words and metaphors with parables, critique, tales of love and misfortune. It was pure magic and I clung to the side of the stage, filming with my hair on fire. We were tired and sunburnt at the end of the day but counted ourselves lucky.

STORYTELLING
Finding music during these first days in Tana had not been easy. Apart from a couple of nightclubs where young prostitutes hunt for older French tourists, Antananarivo was dark and dull at night. In this city of millions there was not even a regular cinema. And so, most evenings, Hanitra, Njaka, Parissa and I sat by the fireplace in the dining room, sometimes jamming, but more than often entertaining each other with stories. Njaka, who did not speak English nor French, was the silent listener. Hanitra was the star of the show, a harlequin and an impersonator, a female Al Jolson, a chocolate-coloured Marcel Marceau. With an irrepressible look on her face she regarded Parissa, Njaka and me, eyes wide open beneath the yellow woollen headband she wore over her ears:

'Have you seen all the zebu horns in the rooms and on the walls of Antshow?'

Of course we all had. They were almost everywhere.

'Zebu are sacred. They are here to safeguard me. They are here because of the curse.'

A cold draft blew in through the gap beneath the door. She moved over to the fire.

'When I was born, an ombiasy predicted that I would bring bad luck. The villagers deliberated what to do. Some said that I should be put to death. Others advocated a trial. So they laid me before the gate of a corral. Inside the enclosure were thirty powerful zebus. They threw the gate open and set the zebus loose.'

She paused for effect and made a loud rumbling noise, hammering her hands on the mantelpiece.

'There was a stampede. By miracle I wasn't trampled. I was alive.'

'What happened?' exclaimed Parissa.

'Everyone declared that I was a sorceress. The cattle had protected me. That is why the walls of Antshow, my house, are decorated with zebu horns.'

Concocting props out of lumps of wood from the fireplace and out of the dancing figurines and kitsch tourist memorabilia that littered the shelves of the dining room Hanitra had Parissa, Njaka and I in stitches with her hilarious pantomimes of the rivalries between the great African divas, Mali's Oumou Sangare, South Africa's Sibonghile Khumalo and Cameroun's Sally Nyolo, with whom Hanitra had toured throughout Europe and Africa. An effigy of a chameleon got the part of the larger-than-life Queen of Wassoulou music, Oumou Sangare. One story led to another. The fire crackled, the room turned quiet when she recalled the day Tarika was stranded in New York city. The day was September 11, 2001.

From a hotel room window the band had witnessed the aerial assault on the World Trade Centre. She described the collapse of the towers seen from her bedroom and the horror and panic it had caused in the hotel. All flights over American territory were cancelled. The mighty United States went into emergency status. The promoters decided to forfeit the tour. Hanitra, never one to take things lying down, fought back, insisting the tour proceed by road. The opening concert was to be held in Houston, Texas. While Americans watched their screens in disbelief as the twin towers kept tumbling down every ten minutes on CNN, five Malagasy musicians and their road crew drove south to bring their happy music to a traumatised nation. They zigzagged from coast to coast across the USA. Reactions were mixed. Some boycotted the shows, suspecting that these merry coffee-coloured folks singing in a strange tongue might be celebrating Muslims. Others admired their 'true American' spirit, which declares that 'the show must go on'.

Tarika became a major World Music act, climbing to the top of the World Music charts. Time magazine voted the band amongst the ten best bands in the world. They were in the company of U2 and Radiohead. While the crowds danced, Hanitra's lyrics talked of the neglect of the poor, the disadvantages of being a woman, the corruption of politicians, the sad state of the environment, racism and the legacies of colonialism. Her travels and research around Madagascar provided her with constant new material. There are few female bandleaders in Africa.

Njaka's personal history too was legendary. He was a skinny, long-haired heavy metal guitarist with no money when he first appeared at Antshow to help construct the décor for one of the exhibitions held at the centre. On some of my red-eye photos he looks like a well-known Transsylvanian count's cousin from Djakarta with his protruding teeth and lemur-like eyes. Njaka's favourite band was Iron Maiden. He had been ignorant of Malagasy traditional music but Hanitra had recognised his talent, employed him and veered him towards the time-honoured instruments. He had become a master of the valiha, the kabosy and the marovany—a large rectangular box-like instrument with strings on either side. Whereas the valiha has an ethereal sound that darts with the light-legged bounce of an antelope, the marovany is a black panther on the prowl.

Ever since that exhibition Njaka had remained at Antshow, sleeping in a room down the corridor from us. He was a sweet and considerate guy, a fantastic musician, a little reserved, but that reserve is a Malagasy trait, and the etiquette prohibits the vazaha from prying too much. He had just returned from his first trip out of the island, accompanying Hanitra to Norway to present a play that she had written about Fartein Valen, a Norwegian composer, son of missionaries, who had lived in Madagascar during the late 1800s. Norway is an expensive country and they both roughed it, living on shrimps, rice and chillies in their hotel rooms. One night they were invited to a dinner. They arrived in their street clothes to dine with the king of Norway. Njaka was going places.

Hanitra is a sharp dresser. She struts in a stylish black suit and high heels at a press conference, dances in sexy hot pants on stage, stars in intimate acoustic concerts at Antshow dressed like the Queen of Sheba. Queen bee she surely is: a queen who has assembled an entourage around her of cooks, servants, musicians and people she has trained for tasks she has little time for. From small beginnings she has built an empire, castle and all. Hanitra makes the merry-go-round spin. 'A large bird has a small egg,' goes the Malagasy saying and she has become a big bird indeed. Everyone in Tana knows her. Promoters, politicians, artists, diplomats and expatriates solicit her time. Tantalising offers and interesting projects always arrive. If they don't, she makes them happen, sneaking off on a field trip to unearth old music in the back country or to explore the treasures of the great red island: dinosaur remains, carved wooden portals from 17th century Arab traders, rituals and lore.

The days were busy for all of us, but at night the pace of this enormous city slowed right down. While the fire blazed and the highland wind whistled and whined through the gaps in the doors and windows Hanitra taught us about local customs, places and music to explore on the island, precautions to take and the political and artistic gossip of the capital. One night after retiring, Parissa and I were kept awake, not by the usual fierce dogfights and noisy flushing system of Antshow, but by furious drum rhythms and haunting electric guitar riffs that drifted in and out of our dreams. The music was still pounding when the morning sun broke through the haze. I was intrigued and wanted to check it out, but Hanitra told me that it was a famadihana, a reburial ceremony, and that I could not attend without an invite.

The famadihana is a most peculiar Malagasy tradition. Every few years, when affordable, a family will dig up the remains of their ancestors from their grave. These will then be wrapped in straw mats or cloth and carried around in ecstatic celebrations that can last for days. There is much drinking and dancing. A zebu will be sacrificed to honour the razana. Perhaps the ancestor will return a favor. Family members might hold the skeletal remains in their arms, and sometimes mother, father and the kids are photographed with the bones of grandfather, because for the Malagasy people, the ancestors have never left. After much partying and asking for the ancestors' blessings the remains are re-wrapped in newly woven lambas and reburied. It is a raucous and cathartic event and to witness a famadihana was one of the main reasons I had come to Madagascar. But however much I pestered Hanitra and her dad to attend such an event, I was unsuccessful.*

'Be patient' she said.

A PRESS CONFERENCE

I had been plucking my guitar in the feeble morning sun on the balcony of our room, looking out over the rural scene at the edge of the city: people tilling patches of watercress, cabbage and greens among smatterings of banana trees and basic dwellings; zebus in a swamp and ducks on a pond; women hanging up the laundry on a fence line. Kids whirled up the dust playing soccer on red dirt terraces carved from the hillside. Strings of drifting smoke climbed towards a church steeple on the hill and merged with the bruise-tinted, rainless clouds beyond. In the street below

---

*Our participation in a famadihana is described in my book 'Dancing with the Bones' (2021)

people wrapped in jackets, jumpers and bonnets, cradling babies, balancing baskets of fruit and huge bundles of charcoal on their heads, glanced up with a smile and waved at me. I could not get over the friendliness and dignified courteousness of the locals.

I had taken a couple of Malagasy guitar lessons from Sandy and, while I practiced the quadrille malgache and grappled with the syncopated tsapiky and salegy rhythms, Parissa warmed up her voice in the bathroom. When Parissa and Hanitra harmonised together the superstars in their pictures on the dining room walls listened. I had no voice, but what a thrill it would be to accompany them. I was sure that the concert would be a success. Our songs had taken on exotic new flavours. The chef had thrown red chillies and vanilla in the stew. My song 'Zimbabwe Zimbabwe' was rocking to a different beat with Son on bass kabosy, Njaka on valiha, Hanitra on talking drum and Parissa on kaimbo rambo, a small handheld broom that made a shuffling, rasping sound when rubbed with both hands. Hanitra's take on Parissa's 'Don't Trust the Enemy' which she moaned in a low voice, was hilarious and Njaka added a rocking riff on his lina to 'Yellow Land', a song which Parissa had written about the drought and deforestation in the Australian state of Victoria, now revamped as a jungle romp at an orangutan hoedown in Borneo.

Downstairs the dining room was being decorated with vases and banners for the afternoon's press conference, promoting our joint concert. How our reality had changed since arriving in Madagascar. Contact with our former life and friends was non-existent. There was no internet at

Press conference: Parissa, Carl, Hanitra, Njaka

Antshow. No newspapers. The barrage of war reports from the Lebanese crisis had faded. It was as if the rest of the world had ceased to exist. We communicated in a different tongue with a different race, played alien music with strange instruments. It was an odd, but fabulous feeling. Hanitra, Njaka, Parissa and I lunched on shrimp and red rice while Antshow's staff was rearranging the dining room, adorning the tables with bouquets of flowers. The scruffy fellow, whose task it was to swing open the heavy iron gate at any hour of the day or night, locked up the ferocious guard dog. I always thought that the job of gatekeeper must be very boring. Like an elevator attendant or those good ladies in Brussels, dressed in starched white, who must mind the toilets all day. A shit of a job. The gatekeeper must have felt so too, because a while later he just left without a farewell.

Even before the journalists started dribbling through the gate, a white woman in a designer suit was delivered in a latest model Chevrolet. She wore high heels, nylon stockings and serious make up. The corporate look. She tiptoed up the driveway as if walking on broken glass. Hanitra came down the stairs to greet her. Ms Sullivan was the cultural attaché of the US Embassy. We were introduced and Francia, Hanitra's shy young secretary, offered her an aperitif. She chose a coke. Hanitra herself was groomed like a pedigree cat at a cat show. She had just spent the morning with her hairdresser. She wore fine Italian shoes and a long black coat over a black outfit. Her blouse was embossed with pearls. She was the perfect hostess, the master of ceremonies, the keeper of the castle, leading her guests through the studio, concert hall and dining room, now transformed into a pressroom. All the journalists received red caps with Hanitra's profile. Standing in the courtyard beneath the zebu horns on the walls, she entertained them with her story of the curse and the stampeding cattle. Cameras flashed. We all settled down in the dining room and the interview started.

There were perhaps a dozen journalists, men and women, all wearing their new caps, sitting on benches and chairs, close together. The dining room/press room now appeared more like a classroom. Hanitra charmed the assembly with a few words in English, then told her stories in Malagasy. When it was our turn it soon became apparent that not all journalists understood English so well. Parissa gave a little introduction that was met with blank stares. From the back of the room Ms Sullivan smiled benignly at the journalists, as if to prod them on. Was some American cultural sponsorship involved, I wondered.

'Why do boomerangs come back?' asked a brave woman.

I left it to Parissa. A man without a voice is not much use at a press conference. Parissa tried to demonstrate in the small space how to throw a boomerang with one of her clapsticks, without wounding a journalist, or worse, an American diplomat. She beat clapstick rhythms and warbled 'Ging gang gooli gooli gooli gooli wash wash', while tap dancing. Big applause.

'That's my girl!' I thought. 'Try to stop her.'

'What is the relationship between the kangaroo and your lifestyle?' asked a serious man.

Difficult question. I helped myself to a biscuit while Parissa was tangling herself in an explanation that was incomprehensible to everyone, including myself.

Parissa saved the day by crooning 'Inanay', a pretty song by a group of three Aboriginal women, Lou, Sally and Amy, who called themselves Tiddas.

'How many tribes are in Australia?' a moustachioed man enquired.

Really, you have to be an academic to do these press conferences. Parissa went for the life raft and sang 'Waltzing Matilda'. Massive applause.

'Now you sing something for us,' she requested.

They stood up as one and, with a solemn expression, burst into a Merina song in three-part harmony. It gave us goosebumps.

THE CONCERT

How the return of boomerangs was explained in the newspapers I never knew. All Malagasy papers were in Malagasy.

'Tickets are selling,' Francia assured us.

She was pouring me a second cup of black coffee. I was barely awake, and Sandy had already mounted the PA system in the hall. He was testing the microphone levels:

'Un deux. Un deux.'

I stuck my head in after breakfast. Njaka and Solo were plugging in a marovany and half a dozen valihas—a tangle of leads all over the stage. Parissa and I retired to our room upstairs for a warm-up and returned with our instruments. The sound check took all morning. Sandy was doing a fine job at the desk. We played through some songs in various combinations, worked out some difficult sections. Hanitra explained the running order of the concert. She had printed song titles out on her computer and stuck them to the front of the stage. Lunch was served: fish, spinach, rice and a spicy side dish of red cabbage; a banana for desert. Hanitra gave instructions to her staff and then she and Parissa disappeared upstairs to do their make up and get dressed. The boys were setting up the lights in the concert space, while the Antshow staff ladies decorated the stage with Tarika posters, placed the chairs in neat rows, stocked the bar and set up a table for the merchandise. It was a good time for me to escape, to go clear my head and spare my voice.

Antshow sits on a hill on the outskirts of Tana, above a green valley of fields and peasant houses. I crossed the street and hiked down the hillside, following the narrow tracks of dirt between the fields, where women stepped in single file, thick bundles of grasses on their heads. Women hoeing in neat patches of young growth and men driving zebus looked a little surprised, but were quick to flash a smile when I called out 'manao ahoana'. Chickens ran across the path. A snake slipped away into the tall grass. There are no dangerous snakes in Madagascar. I followed the edge of the lake that bordered the presidential palace, soaking up the pastoral peace, the absence of cars and diesel fumes. Fishermen waved. Two kingfishers flew low over the water. I had to get back.

Well-dressed people were already sipping wines and conversing in the courtyard when I arrived. Ms Sullivan rushed over to greet me. She was wearing a charcoal evening dress, a white Kashmiri shawl draped over her shoulders. She had bought a CD and wanted me to sign it. I mingled among the artists, bureaucrats, musicians, French expatriates and their wives, foreign diplomats and local

THE QUEEN OF MALAGASY MUSIC

elite, nodding and smiling. This was not going to be a barn dance for the poor folks down in the valley. No one tried to talk with me. Someone must have already passed on the news that I was a mute. Journalists who had been present at the press conference greeted me like old friends. Upstairs Parissa was touching up her mascara. Hanitra was nowhere in sight. I retired to the dining room to sit by the wood fire where I kept Hanitra's parents company until it was show time.

Solo and Njaka opened the evening with an instrumental tune named 'Afindrafindrao', also known as the quadrille malgache. This tune, based on the French quadrille dance, was popularised in the Merina courts during the 19th century. These days it is often played at the beginning of social events on the Hauts Plateaux and it was the first Malagasy guitar piece that Sandy had taught me. The quadrille that was introduced into the Festa Junina in Brazil* had also made it to Madagascar. The rippling tinkle of the two valihas soothed the audience like a windup music box. The lights dimmed. Hanitra entered the stage in a gold and rose-coloured knee-length silken dress over a pair of pyjamas of the same material with tight cuffs around the ankles. A pink scarf hung from her shoulders. The queen of Malagasy music looked like a tantric deity, a sky-dancing Dakini. She picked up her talking drum, the tama, that she had acquired when recording Tarika's hit album, *Son Egal*, with Senegalese guest musicians. Tapping her feet in elegant, golden, oriental slippers she let her voice soar. The coloured beads

---

*more about the Festa Junina in my book *Dancing with the Bones* (2021)

of her silver bracelets sparkled in the stage lights. On the wall behind her, polished zebu horns watched over her. The sorceress invoked the spirits.

While Hanitra was a sky-dancing Tibetan goddess, Parissa had turned into the nimble-footed Greek nymph Aphrodite, born of the froth of waves. She darted across the stage, charmed the audience in her own jargon of English, French, Spanish and Malgash, and sang like the South American patativa bird, renowned for its beautiful song. Patativa was the name Brazilian admirers, in awe of her voice, had bestowed on her. The Antshow crowd loved her. She crooned my new tune, 'All Alone', with such coy intimacy that, after a silence of suspended breaths, everyone erupted into thunderous applause. On request she sang a Greek song. Solo did a solo spot, Hanitra revealed two new compositions and I backed the Antshow Queen on 'Fony Ianao Mbolakely', with the pretty guitar part I had so sweated over. Njaka's rippling marovany plucking –at once furious and delicate- raised the hairs on my arms. Striking his phallic-necked lina he burst into 'Yellow Land', head banging, his shiny long black hair swirling round his shoulders, his heavy metal past not quite forgotten. This rocking blues, in which a blond haired Greek-Australian woman channels John Lee Hooker, brought down the house. It was the kind of song the Malagasy expected from vazaha. The quintessential, dirty growl of Muddy Waters, Creedance Clearwater and ACDC. We were firing. People danced in the aisles.

'Encore!'

'Encore!'

'More! More!'

Someone shouted 'Yellow Land' and we responded with another Australian-Malagasy heavy metal remix as the house lights went on.

Drinks and nibbles were served at the bar. Parissa, Hanitra and I signed CDs and conversed with well-wishers. We were photographed with members of the audience. Daddy Rasoanaivo, his beaming wife by his side, shook my hand warmly, abandoning his Malagasy reserve.

'He is moved,' said his daughter.

After everyone had left, the gatekeeper locked the castle and set the guard dog loose. Hanitra opened a bottle of Malagasy coconut rum and the musicians unwound at the bar. By 11.30 pm it was all over. The Malagasy like an early night. The curtains were closed and my voice needed to rest. And after all this, we didn't perform 'Put your Hand in Mine' the song that started it all.

18
VAZAHA AND VEZO

Parissa and I sat in the dust waiting for the taxi brousse to depart for Saint Augustin. This was a larger and sturdier truck than the common mini vans, its wooden walls painted coral red and vivid blue. 'Red for the earth, blue for the Malagasy sky,' I thought. Roads are rough in the south of Madagascar. Journeys can take days. Passengers sat beside their bundles and baskets in the harsh sun, chattering and arguing, while two men heaved crates of beer on to the roof, furniture, ever scarcer tree poles, bicycles, bags of cement, rolls of grass matting and raffia baskets bulging with fruit, vegetables and chickens. A mother deloused a child, another woman plaited her companion's hair, tying it in two neat buns on the top, with swift movements of her fingers. A child played with a young chicken, hugging it like a doll. Vendors hawked sweet buns and meat. It was all very 'mora mora', slow and easy.

Two hours later we boarded. The bus was fitted with wooden benches on a metal frame, so close together you could not fit your knees between them. The floor beneath our feet was stacked with bags of flour and manioc, wood for construction and more crates of beer. There were no windows, just iron bars. The women tied scarfs over their heads to protect their hair from the dust. The sand blew right through the bus as we bounced on the rutted track, sliding through the loose sand, almost getting stuck in a ditch to let a zebu cart pass, the passengers tossed about, holding on. Loud tsapiky music cracked through the speakers. The music was hot and everyone in the bus was so friendly that a rather uncomfortable trip turned into a joy ride. We were heading for Sarodrano, a village of Vezo fishermen, south of Tuléar.

Since there was no bus to Sarodrano, we had been told to get off at Ambanilia and walk from there. But Ambanilia was just a spot amongst the thorny shrubs and rocks in the middle of nowhere, high above the sea. All the friendly passengers waved and shouted 'veloma' as we started marching down the rugged track that the driver had pointed to. It was midday and bloody hot, not an inch of shade. Parissa and I trudged, sweating under our rucksacks, down towards the sea. There was no sign of habitation. We hiked for an hour or so until the rocks turned to sand and we found ourselves in a weird forest of thorn-covered truncheons, leafless trees of intricately patterned branches, giant cactus-like plants with towering tentacles like elephant trunks covered in killer spikes. This was the Alluaundia procerans, the extraterrestrial vegetation of southern Madagascar. Andrea would call them 'arbres pleuvier' and the villagers 'sono'. "Arbres de cauchemar," he would say, 'trees from a nightmare'. We kept on going until we reached the hut of a fisherman on the beach. He offered to take us to Sarodrano in his pirogue, a dugout canoe with an outrigger and a sail, but since we would have to wait for the tide to rise, we continued plodding along the beach. Sarodrano lies at the tip of a sandy peninsula that juts out into the ocean.

We arrived at our destination, Andrea's huts, in the late afternoon. He wasn't there, but a caretaker showed us to a cabin, thatched with grass and reeds, a verandah on three sides. Grass matting covered a raised wooden floor. It had a small bathroom of the bucket-and-can variety. The dunes right behind the hut served as toilets. There was no electricity. Parissa and I jumped into the sea. Then we collapsed on the bed and tuned into the gurgling patter of the wavelets, splashing five metres from our hut. We were the only guests in paradise.

It was Hanitra who had told us about Andrea's place. Andrea was an Italian from Genoa, the son of Sardinian parents. He had been in Madagascar for twenty years. Eighteen years ago he had arrived in Sarodrano and had never left. The place was unspoilt; there were no mosquitoes by the sea; the Vezo were friendly. Andrea had built a few huts, away from the village, for the few visitors that managed to get here. It provided him with a small income and stimulation. Otherwise he read and went fishing with the Vezo.

I sat writing my diary at a crudely made table in the last rays of the sun sinking into the waters of the Strait of Mozambique, when Andrea and two other fishermen pulled a pirogue past the tide mark, up on the beach. The men folded the sail and Andrea greeted us while handing the catch of fish and crabs to three Vezo women from the village. One lit a fire on the sand. The others started cleaning the fish.

That night we enjoyed a feast of raw fish with carrots, fried calamari and huge crabs from the mangroves. Andrea uncorked a bottle of white wine to celebrate our arrival and entertained us with tales of his life among the Vezo. He was a fount of local lore and gossip. It was a surreal welcome in a surreal place. A banquet for three by gaslight, in a hut decorated with Malagasy drawings, maps, masks, fishing spears, wooden sculptures, treasures from the sea, a poster from a Malagasy music festival and rows of books, most of them in Italian. The sharp-teethed jawbone of a shark leered at us from the shadows.

We woke up on the beach of Eden. Fishermen sailed close to shore and waved. This was the place I had in mind when I wrote the song 'Sailing on Perfect Time' at the start of the journey. I slipped into the sea. Everything was golden and blue. Sea, sky and sand. Parissa joined me. We frolicked, blissed out in the lukewarm Indian Ocean, and strolled along the water's edge, village children in tow. 'Cadeau vazaha! Cadeau!' Parissa made their requests into a song: 'tis cadeau, tis cadeau.' Instantly they all joined in and soon Parissa and the kids were dancing wildly on the beach, Parissa's towel serving as a lamba, which they held around the waist as they, each in turn, demonstrated their prowess at the hip-and-groin thrust. I traced faces in the sand and the kids drew palm trees, a pirogue, a fish and a crab. We strolled over to the village, played soccer with the boys. The soccer ball was made from rags and tied with fishing line. We climbed over the dunes to the mudflats. The tide had already cleansed the village toilet. Girls were singing while collecting pipis in a bucket. Old men were mending nets. Two small boys were floating a toy pirogue. Most of the menfolk, and many women too, were out fishing. The sun was almost right above us.

These tranquil days in Sarodrano were our first chance to wind down after weeks of arduous travelling in search of music and rituals. Four framed, faded photographs hung on the grass wall of our hut. A grey weathered cupboard with carved panels stood beside a small bamboo table with three candles and seashells. Above the bed hung a linen sheet to prevent bits of grass falling on us while we slept. Wooden shutters kept out the sun, the sand and wind. The dwelling was squeezed between the ocean and the dunes. The ocean reached into our cabin with its constant swishing of wavelets, its salty air and sculpted treasures. In the heat of the day we watched postcard pirogues paddling past the window, while drowsing on our bed. The days always ended with the western sunsets over the strait.

Never in our lives had we been so relaxed. It was a fantasy life, but who was complaining? We practiced yoga on the beach and I did my first gentle vocal exercises. My voice was slowly healing. I loved the solitude. No diesel smoke, no screaming radio, no rumbling generator, no road to the door. All the cooking was done on a woodfire on the beach. The three fierce-looking Vezo cooks, their hair platted in nuggets that gave them a Mickey Mouse like appearance, stewed spiced crayfish to die for, then watched us tear the claws apart; three woman of polished ebony in faded dresses sprawling on the yellow sand, as the sun went down.

I found some anthropology books in French, frayed at the edges, and read about the ancestor worship amongst the Mahafaly and Antandroy. Their elaborately carved and painted tombs were often larger than their houses. Antandroy protocol forbids a son to live in a house larger than his father's. If the grandfather should still be alive, this would make living arrangements for a young Antandroy family of traditional bent, rather cramped. I found a yellowish book entitled 'Civilisation de Madagascar – art et archéologie, anthropologie sociale' and read about a Betsimiseraka slave who was sold many times from master to master before the great rebellion against the French. Lazing on the verandah, I learned the fate of Gaspar de San Bernardino, a Franciscan monk who was shipwrecked on the West coast of Madagascar in 1606. I became absorbed in the intrigues, web of alliances and conflicts between the Portuguese, the Arabs and the Sakalava kings in centuries past. These were slow days in Sarodrano. We were idling in first gear. A comatose, flea-ridden dog was permanently lodged on the back verandah. A puppy choked on a crab. A hen jumped on the stool beside me. The tide was receding. The pirogues were coming in. The moon rose in a pale lavender sky. The sea turned ashen. Tumbling waves and whimpering wind. The Milky Way. I fell into deep sleep.

While Parissa read Jean-Paul Sartre –'In this place?'– I ambled across the dunes to the village school. Three buildings stood on a stretch of shell-gritted sand, bare but for one shady tree and a Malagasy flag, flapping on a pole. The director showed me around the five classrooms. Each time we entered all the children jumped up and yelled 'bonjour monsieur!' I, in turn, introduced myself, asked their names and played teacher, making kids write Roman numerals on the blackboard and asking them what the words were in French and Malagasy. I met the other teachers and heard about the lack of books and pencils. There were two hundred and fifty children at this school. Through lack of space they were rotating: some came in the morning, others in the afternoon. I wanted to contribute, but there were no shops in Sarodrano. Tuléar was a world away. I vowed to travel with a supply of pencils. I gave a donation to the school coffers. 'Au revoir monsieur!'

One day we walked over to the townlet of Saint Augustin, an old pirate haven, and rowed a canoe up the Onilahy river. When we returned the wind blew strong over the ocean and the sun was sinking low. To spare us the return hike, we boarded a pirogue and two Vezo boys raced across the waves all the way back to Sarodrano. The Vezo are born seafarers. Even small children are skilled at navigating pirogues. Each pirogue had a crew of two: while one steered, the other did a balancing act, leaning over the outrigger and changing the sail. It was a game between man, wind and sail, an exhilarating trip. What had taken us half a day to walk, took half an hour by sea.

I had asked Andrea whether there were any musicians in the village. I knew that most villages had a band of young kabosy players for festive and other occasions. Andrea called the kabosy 'mandoliny', a word often used in the south. He let it be known in the village that I was interested in hearing them play. The band was keen and told him that they would come over to play for us tonight.

'I leave you in charge,' he said, 'I must go to the village to treat a sick child.' Though Andrea was not a doctor, he was the only long-time vazaha here with access to foreign medicine, and he had come to fulfill that function.

It was a night of nights. Solid darkness. No moon yet, only a faraway glimmer of stars, impenetrable for an addict of the sixty-watt light bulb, but the locals have become used to moving about in the dark. In the main hut, the white light of the gas lamp hissed above the table where Parissa and I were reading and writing, waiting for dinner. Outside on the beach, the cooks sat in the sand around two pots bubbling on a wood fire. We heard a racket of chatter, laughter and yells coming from the dunes and then our hut was surrounded by a gabble of voices in the invisible night. I stepped out in the dark and immediately fell over a mob of children sitting in the sand. Everyone shrieked and laughed. I called out a greeting. A chorus answered 'Salaama!' 'The whole village has come along to the party,' I thought. I squatted and saw the silhouette of a kabosy player, hunched over in the sand. What was he doing? I wished I could see something. Following the dunes like a blind man I stumbled back to our hut to find my torch and camera.

Everyone was overexcited. It is that southern hemisphere keg of dynamite, waiting for a spark. I stepped over screaming kids and crawled amongst legs, arms and bodies, to find the musicians. Why were they not playing? I shone my torch on a kabosy. Three young men were carving tuning pegs from a piece of driftwood. I squatted beside them pointing a beam of light at their knives. The fourth guy was already banging a small drum with a large mallet. It seemed like a shonky drum, but made a deep booming thump. The tallest man stood up and played a fast riff on a rough square box with three strings. The kids screamed and instantly got up to dance. I shouted for Parissa to help me, holding the torch while I filmed. It was too dark, but filming was the only way to record the music. There was a lot of push and shove. Children and adults pulled her into the dance. The beam of light bounced off a face, an arm, settled on a strumming hand, flashed white eyes in a black face. I held on to the camera and let it roll.

'The guy on the ground!' I yelled.

'Doing my best,' said Parissa.

One boy sat in the sand with a bass kabosy, the size of a suitcase, thumbing fast slides up the fretboard and hammering the soundbox with his wrist. Another one strummed a counterpoint to the lead player on a one-stringed instrument. Party at my house again. This was great. The sullen cooks were standing in the doorway with an annoyed look on their faces. Seeing that no one was about to stop after an hour of mayhem, I paid the lead player five thousand ariary and thanked him for the music. The relieved cooks served dinner and I went back inside.

But no one went away. We dined while the mob settled all around the hut, the windows and doors framed with faces, watching us eat. Bass and drums kept the beat going. I hadn't realised that this was just the chill-out part of the night, until the other kabosy players returned. They had gone to the village to buy rum with my money. They were fired up and now the party commenced for real. The band was cooking, the villagers dancing in the dark. Meanwhile we chewed on crabs inside the hut. A bizarre scene it was: a well-mannered dinner party in the bright gaslight and delirious chaos in the black night.

A boisterous woman named Paulette, whom must have had her fair share of rum, waltzed inside, goading us to dance. I followed Paulette outside and boogied in the sand. The musicians played twice as well now that the pack was romping. Parissa joined in. There was no way this party was going to stop any time soon. The moon rose, the wind settled down and the fandango shifted to the front of the hut. The crowd had grown even larger. I noticed a mob of women huddled together on the beach that I hadn't noticed before. Paulette grabbed me again and we jived by the seashore. Vazaha and Vezo rocking the night away. Paulette sang, a young kid rapped, drums and kabosy players ripped up the beach. Crabs and fishes, the joint was jumping. Around midnight I thanked everyone. The Vezo retired to their village, the vazaha to their cabin. All that remained was the splashing of the sea and the chirps of the gecko in our hut.

19

THE MAN IN THE LIME-GREEN SUIT / TARAB IN MAJUNGA

I have dedicated a whole book to my search for Tarab, that Arabic word for the elusive ecstasy that can overcome one when moved by poetry or music. It has been an evergreen fig tree among the saplings of my personal woods. Henri Salvador did it to me as a child, so did the boy scout skifflers, the French chansonniers, Buddy Holly, my blues and folk heroes, the African musicians, traditional or modern, the raga queens and the many more to follow who would give me goosebumps, bringing me to tears or euphoria, leaving their imprint on who I am.

I found it in unexpected places, like in a cheap open-air amphitheatre in La Paz, Bolivia, where, one Sunday afternoon, an array of Quechua village bands performed their wild and sorrowful huayno tunes of abandoned love, tragedy and thwarted desire. Raw-hearted songs, songs that have nothing more to lose, songs to cleanse your soul with. A bowler-hatted and triple-skirted woman sang her heart out in a shrill voice that pierced the shroud of accordion, guitar, mandolin, charango or violin, all huddled around the one microphone. Between her feet, or dangling from her hand, a bottle of pisco fanned the flames of fervour as the sun sank over the Altiplano. I sat in a trance on the concrete stairs while my four-year old son played with the other kids around the stage, running up and down the steps among the sellers of ice cream, empanadas and lemonade.

In contrast, but just as gripping, was the delicate, breathtaking artistry of the Vietnamese orchestra that accompanied the traditional water puppetry in a Hanoi theatre with cymbals, bells, bamboo flutes, drums, upright violins, hammered dulcimers and achingly bowed monochords, pulling my eyes away from the magic craft of the puppeteers towards the balconies on either side with the orchestra, my tears flowing to a slap-stick ancient rural folk tale.

The soundtrack of life is a six-lane highway with countless exits leading to interesting destinations. Tarab experiences come by surprise and none more so than the encounter in the harbour of Majunga on the west coast of Madagascar with the man in a lime-green suit.

Parissa and I left Ankarafantsika a little after dawn and sat by the side of the Route National 4. We flagged down a taxi brousse half an hour later, sharing three seats with six people. Soon a child had thrown up on my leg and removed my glasses. I couldn't do anything about it. My foot was numb, jammed between a car battery, heavy luggage and a big woman's leg. A bag of cassava and the big woman's hip snared my arms. After a while she put her face, covered in masonjoany (a face pack made from wood and water), on my shoulder and fell asleep. We narrowly avoided a truck and almost lost Parissa when the door suddenly flew open.

But everyone was in a good mood. We were all one happy family on the road to Majunga and there was some terrific music blaring from the crackly speakers.

'Dadah de Fort Dauphin,' shouted the driver.

'Must try to find a recording,' I thought.

'Tsanga tsangana,' ('we are only going for a promenade') Parissa asserted with a smile, fending off a platoon of pouse-pousse drivers as we strutted to the hotel Chez Chableaux. We were in Majunga, the major town for the northern Sakalava people, and also the town of choice of Antananarivo's middle class fleeing the wintry highlands to enjoy a holiday by the beach. The Sakalava are, together with the Bara, the most African of the Malagasy people. They practice spirit possession, keeping protective relics and amulets. The Sakalava occupy much of the West coast of Madagascar and are skilled seafarers. Much feared in the past, they raided the faraway Comoro islands and the East African coast in large fleets of outrigger canoes to capture slaves.

Majunga has strong connections with East Africa. Shops of Arab and Indian traders lined the streets. There was a small white mosque opposite our hotel. Beyond Majunga's skyline the Indian Ocean shimmered in the light of noon. Ships on the harbour slumbered in the heat. We found a roadside stall and dined on zebu kebabs, manioc patties, samosas and coconut pancakes. Streams of gaudy pousse-pousse trotted by. Minibuses, trucks and the better quality vehicles of holidaymakers competed for space. A boy pushed a cart, too heavy for a man. We reached the ocean and sat in the shade of a thick baobab tree. It was three hundred years old and a sign warned that it was 'fady' (taboo) to touch this sacred tree, though many had carved their name in its trunk. We strolled along the promenade by the sea and tumbled into the fair that would make my day.

Near the docks, on the grounds behind the seashore promenade, rows of market stalls displayed clothes and fabrics, low-priced Malagasy VCDs made in China, woven baskets, craftwork carved from zebu horn, snacks and drinks, dried fish and live goats. A dense throng of locals and holidaymakers from Tana shuffled among the stalls. Banners fluttered in the breeze. A stage had been erected with a bright red canopy and advertisements boomed from the speakers. A compère walked on and made announcements in Malagasy. A troupe of young women stepped on to the hard red dirt in front of the stage, clapping sticks and singing. An intricate, silvery pattern graced their faces; white flowers dazzled in shiny black hair. They all wore white lambas with a florid pattern, knotted above the breasts. A scarf of the same material was stretched diagonally across the shoulder. A man brought a microphone stand, while the girls sang and swayed with coordinated bows and graceful movements of the hips, now and then squatting or breaking into dance steps. The crowd gathered around them in a tight circle, children sitting on the ground, adults standing behind, looking over each other's shoulders. Spectators climbed the balustrade of the promenade to get a better view. Behind them white sailing boats dotted the Mozambique Channel.

The next troupe walked on. These women were dressed in red and white lambas. A wizened man, a cigarette dangling from his mouth, pumped a beat-up accordion, held by a scarf around his neck. A skinny fellow beat a complex rhythm on a handheld shaker, a katsa or katra, against the palm of his hand, in time with the steps of the dancers. Several of the girls wore masonjoany paste on their faces. Older women and shy teenage girls sang together in a call and response fashion. They drew tiny circles with their hands and, each time they bent backwards, with their arms held high, the audience roared with approval.

I craned over a woman's shoulders to record and film. This was antsa music, the traditional songs of the Sakalava that had given rise to the dance-floor-burning salegy style with its driving bass and drums in fast 6/8 time, polyphonic vocals, funky accordion or keyboards, electric guitars that ring like bells. I had played the salegy tunes of the great Sakalava bands for my students at Southern Cross University: Jaojoby, Jerry Marcoss, The Jaguars. But I wasn't prepared for what came next.

Nine women came shuffling out onto the dirt, clapping their hands in complex patterns that reminded me of gypsy performers. These were no shy little girls, but stout adult women, lambas tied around their waists, their feet stamping the ground in flip-flop sandals. A strange-looking little man stepped behind them in a lime-coloured suit, with a lamba tied around his waist of the same white and purple pattern as the women's attire. He wore dark sunglasses, a white shirt beneath his suit, and black leather shoes. His presence marked him as the leader of the troupe. To the side, stood a short accordion player with a permanent grin of pleasure on his face, and a tall, slim young man who strummed a rectangular wooden box with a small sound hole, a thin, long neck with partial frets, strings of fishing wire and nine wooden pegs: a homemade kabosy. Both players wore hats, threadbare tee-shirts and lambas, and were barefoot. The group was fired up, even before the microphone stand could be put in place. They were not attempting to perform. They were doing their thing. For real. Something stirred in my abdomen. I stretched my camera above someone's head and filmed. Two boys climbed up a tree to get a better look.

The women jounced and jerked to the driving rhythm, singing together until one of them broke into an improvised rap while the others clapped, shrieked and ululated. They seesawed, bent backwards and lurched forward, threw their arms up in the air, and beat their chest to the rhythm. The little man in the green suit stepped to the microphone and shouted an avalanche of words. The women yelled as the man bent at the knees and galloped on the spot like a stallion. A tall woman jumped before him, her hands waving, her hips swaying. The others screamed and clapped louder to urge the two dancers on. I was stunned by their energy, mesmerised by their abandon, stirred by their intensity. Were they drunk? In a trance? Was I? Before I came down to earth they had danced off, to make place for another antsa group.

I motioned to Parissa, who had been sitting on the ground between the children, and followed the odd man and his entourage. I had lost interest in anything else that might be going on. By the time we caught up, the group had entered the courtyard of a nearby building. Standing under a rubber tree, the little green man unleashed his raps while all nine women bounced and gyrated around him, whooping and yelping. The commotion was chaotic, the vitality red-hot. The women rolled their eyes, shook their hips, each one of them dancing to her own ecstasy, stamping her feet on the ground like flamenco dancers in Cordoba. The man was in a trance now, hurling his words like a conga player slaps his drums. The women responded with squeals and answered his call 'Zabubwe! Zabubwe!' The accordion player grinned, the kabosy man ran his fingers over the fretboard like a spider on speed.

Only a hundred yards away, on the stage of the fairground, the loudspeakers shrieked announcements. Prizes to be given away; people cheered. But at that moment the centre of Majunga's gravity was here and now, though the few passers-by pointedly ignored it. Were Parissa and I the only ones to respond to this force? A young girl carrying a baby strolled among the dancing troupe. A man stepped out of the building and handed one of the women a banknote. Everyone yodelled. The banknote was stuck between the plaited braids of a pretty dancer with a sky blue blouse. She threw her arms up in the air, ululating; she arched backward ninety degrees, sinews taut, muscles rippling. Were these people possessed? The man in green stood before the donor, declaiming his praises, while pointing him out to people nearby. That little man in the green suit, dressed like the singer of a backyard doowop group, surely was a magnet, a shaman to whom I wanted to give my soul. I was snared.

Parissa had been standing nearby, watching while I filmed until, suddenly, the women invited her in. She was surrounded. Cheering women clapped their hands above their heads as Parissa sang with them: 'Zabubwe! Zabubwe!' A tall woman leapt before her, hips writhing, and stomping her feet. Parissa must dance. A chorus of shrieks and yells. The clapping intensified. The shaman stepped up, held Parissa by the hand and sang to her. She was in tears, sobbing but grinning. My heart too was pounding in my chest. I felt that I had never seen women in this way. I was electrified by their ardor, their explosive power, the intense joy, freedom and abandonment.

But the energy did not relent, the séance went on and on. On high voltage. The music never stopped, the clapping never stopped. The accordion found room to soar. One of the women put her scarf around the shaman who strutted and pranced with two, then three, and then with all of them. He took the handsome woman with the sky blue blouse by the hand and rapped to her. I wished that I could understand what he was saying. He looked into her eyes; she radiated; the others ululated, wiggled and jiggled. They tossed back their heads, dropped into a squat position with hands quivering around their faces. The barrage of speech flew faster. Call and response ignited. Women laid hands on him and on each other, rocked back and forth, pushed out their behinds and stuck out their breasts. I rushed over and handed the man in the lime-green suit a ten thousand ariary note. It was a lot of money, but I couldn't help myself. He grabbed my hand and sang to me. I stopped filming.

Later that night we met with our Malagasy friends from the band Tarika—Hanitra, Njaka and Nous-Nous—and encountered the antsa group once more, still dancing, clapping, singing and yelling in the dark near the market stalls. They were wild, streaming with sweat among a packed crowd. The shaman rapped deliriously and Hanitra translated his stream of consciousness, proverbs and wisdoms about women, work, society and money. Interrupted by a drunk, he sang about the evils of alcohol. I was transfixed. I wanted to be a part of this group. It was all that mattered. How could I leave them? I must follow them, stay in Boina among the Sakalava, dedicate my life to understanding their dialect, sing as they do, dance as they do, levitate! That is what Tarab does to you.

20

A DESERT ISLAND COLLECTION

To warrant lugging a disk to a desert island when your canoe is small, the disk has to fulfill certain conditions. It has to be music that you have listened to many times and still it keeps enchanting you. Some albums you might adore, but you have memorised them so well that they are not worth lugging along. These are already imprinted on your brain cells. The Beatles' *Sergeant Pepper*, Pink Floyd's *Dark Side of the Moon*, Miles Davis' *Kind of Blue*, or anything by ABBA might fall in this category. Others, perhaps, evoke a powerful memory that will take you back, without fail, to a certain state of mind, a cardinal moment in your life. That kind of music you must keep close to you. It has become an integral part of who you are. So here is my batch. It has been revamped by the hour, but it is getting late and a heavy cloud cover has closed the curtains on the secret life of this moonless night. Undeterred, the soundtrack never stops. Listen! Crickets and cicadas in the upper register, the thumping ocean waves at the back of the orchestra, the wind sweeping through like violins bowed by galloping horses, the branches rattling their leaves, dropping driplets. The rain has stopped, the bats are out and I must go to bed. These are the disks that I would lock in a black box to store beneath my bunk, if my boat was leaving tomorrow at daybreak.

1. MATESO *TRIPLE EARTH* (1987)
Bagamoyo College of the Arts featuring Hukwe Zawose

Ivory blonde ringlets of Afro hair creeping from a skullcap, a chubby face framed with a jovial grin, neck beads, an embroidered vest and bulging white pants that made him look more stocky than he was, a djembe always nearby. An affable guy. A cool dude. That was Bernie Hewitt, a white African, born in New Zealand. I met him when he joined the Sydney Choir The Voices from the Vacant Lot, of whom Parissa and I were members, a fun troupe that felt like a family affair, with a repertoire of songs from all over the globe. We briefly formed a quartet with him and his girlfriend Betty but, before long, it fizzled when Parissa and I left the city to study, voice and composition respectively, at Southern Cross University in Lismore on the north coast of New South Wales.

Since then we had formed a band, The Hottentot Party, that had been having considerable success. We had a couple of albums out and were playing festivals, pubs, halls and sport fields when Bernie turned up and joined the band. We rehearsed, had a photo shoot but, for his first show, he arrived beside the stage, crestfallen, with a sorry grimace and a bandaged hand, which he had cut with a saw a few hours before. Bernie's planets were in collision, creating chaos in a life that was running away from him, pulling him in all directions. Amidst a whirlwind of women and lodgings he soon left for Africa, leaving an exhaust of question marks. I never found out anything about his past, and now, thinking back, I am not even sure whether he ever did play a gig with the band after all.

Bernie went to Bagamoyo to study the thumb piano, the ilimba, with the Tanzanian master, Hukwe Zawose and became a fine player himself. In his footsteps some of my friends went over to study with Hukwe as well. But I rarely heard a word from Bernie, just whispers from the grapevine. Bernie was in Europe with Hukwe doing shows. He had connected Hukwe with Peter Gabriel's Real World label. Bernie had met a woman and was settling down in Tanzania. He had a son. And then, all of a sudden, the news that he had organised a little tour Down Under for Hukwe and his nephew Charles and they would give a concert in Byron Bay.

When Parissa and I had first met we had been amazed that we both were fans of João Bosco and Hukwe Zawose. Hukwe already had a mezzanine seat in the Broadway of our hearts. Thus, it was an unreal thrill to be invited to open up for the Tanzanian masters. But who else in Australia had ever heard of Hukwe Zawose? Though unknown to anyone locally, Hukwe and Charles packed the hall with a crowd of four hundred curious people. In our region it is West African music, with its furious djembe dance polyrhythms, its balafons and divine kora harp players, that is the African music of preference. But Africa is a big continent with countless diverse cultures and, like an immense river, it spills out into a giant delta, floating musical barges, catamarans, schooners, steamers and ocean liners with a cargo of traditional and contemporary music styles. I believe that the Tanzanian variety was an ear-opener for many.

Hukwe and Charles stepped on to the stage in a headdress of animal furs, a cape of pelts, a necklace of beads and white feathers, bare-chested, biceps tight under firm straps of fur, holding their ilimbas above grass skirts, feet rooted on muscular legs, bare but for ankle rattlers. Both Charles and him, side by side, ilimbas, the box as wide as their broad shoulders leaning on their bellies, the heavy metal tongues plucked hot and sizzling, the hissing of the spiderwebs covering the sound holes. Instantly the vibe in the hall shifted. You could not escape it. You could not ignore it. Startlingly, Hukwe's shamanistic groan, a voice dug up from deep beneath the ground that made the hairs on the back of your neck stand up, leapt from a low growl into a falsetto of narrative, interspersed with yodels and overtones that seemed to emanate from another creature. It penetrated you like a wooden splinter. Hukwe and Charles were grand. Soul keepers. I believe it was a revelation for many and everyone adored them. Almost everyone.

'When you've heard one song, you've heard them all,' declared our soundman, 'it sounds all the same to me.'

As for Bernie, he returned to Tanzania and the rumours dwindled. We would not see him again for many years.

Although Hukwe Zawose was a master on various instruments, including the bowed iseze and the hammered marimba it is, foremost, the ilimba, the Tanzanian metal-tongued instrument plucked with the thumbs he is known for. The player holds a wooden sound box with attached staggered metal tines and plucks them. Some tines are sympathetic, resonate with the frequencies without being played, which makes the ilimba different from other thumb pianos. All over Africa you will find a vast array of sanzas, small and large, with countless tunings and designs, each culture with its own technique and traditions. Mbira in Zimbabwe, kalimba in Kenya, likembe in the Congo, kadongo in Uganda or the ilimba in Tanzania. All of them can lull and trap you with jarring overtones and polyrhythms, lingering vibrations of adjacent tines, 'a music of murmurs, the opposite of music for competitions, compositions. Instruments to relieve us dreamily from all the noisemakers of this world.' (Henri Michaux -*Facing the Vanishing World*)

Hukwe Zawose has entranced me ever since I heard this album and, that is why he opens this desert island collection.

2. MUSIC FOR 18 MUSICIANS *ECM RECORDS* (1978)
Steve Reich Ensemble

This album has never stopped mesmerising me. It sings, it dances, it never lets you off the hook. Always water cascading over rapids, gazelles scampering in flight, spirits streaking in and out of view, landscapes changing and sudden forks in the road with so many paths to follow, to an industrial site in a metropolis of the future, inside a primeval rainforest in the wet season, at a courtly temple ceremony or a shamanistic rite, until you notice that you have stopped chattering, gone still inside and let yourself be lifted, and transported.

When first released it was a milestone in minimalism, an artform that flowered from the sixties onward, and had at its core a stripping down of a work to its essential elements. Composer Steve Reich made use of repetitive patterns, drones and pulses, slowly changing chords and phase shifting. Though the term minimalism might sound simple, it was far from it. However many times I have heard it, it always sounds new to me. Therefore it travels with me to my desert island. Recently I heard and saw the footage on YouTube of a dazzling live performance of the piece by the Temple University Percussion Ensemble featuring xylophones, marimbas, pianos, clarinets, vibraphone, violin, cello and voices. Strongly recommended.

3. FINA ESTAMPA ÂO VIVO (1995)
Caetano Veloso

For those who are not familiar with the Brazilian composer, singer, writer and activist, Caetano Veloso, I should commence by stating that Caetano is a musical giant and creative force on par with Bob Dylan, Bob Marley and Lennon and McCartney. In an international world of music that has, over the last sixty years, been dominated by the cultural imperialism of the USA, any artist singing in a 'foreign' language faces a barrier, not only of language, but of a general ignorance of the sensibilities of other cultures. We are so used to the testosterone of rock that has pervaded all our popular music that artists like Caetano Veloso or Jacques Brel can seem as much of an acquired taste to many of us, as Indian classical music can be to the adherents of Beethoven and Mozart. Music is about opening your ears.

Whereas the USA imported 650,000 slaves from the African continent, the Portuguese brought close to five million slaves to Brazil—more than any other country. Until a century ago Brazil was mostly a nation of Africans and mulattoes. Although repeated waves of immigrants have changed the ratio and slavery was finally abolished, racial discrimination continues. Whereas white Brazilians dominate in media, politics and business, the darker ones reign the musical and much of the cultural sphere.

Caetano Veloso was born in the state of Bahia, Brazil's most African state, where black culture has been, and is, alive and teeming, fertilising all of Brazil and beyond. As a child Caetano was drawn to music, painting, books and films. At university he studied philosophy. He is an intellectual in a musical universe crowded with pop lightweights with little to say. He is an atheist in a nation riddled with Catholic superstition and evangelical sects. Picasso was Picasso. Caetano is Caetano, uniquely himself. The first bossa nova hit song of the master of the genre, João Gilberto, 'Chega de Saudade', caused an upheaval in Caetano's life. He was seventeen, and bossa nova would remain a major influence for the rest of a career, spanning six decades, more than fifty albums, songs in films, and nine Latin Grammy Awards and two Grammy Awards in the US.

Veloso moved to Rio de Janeiro in the early sixties. He was twenty. In hindsight I can see destiny waiting for him. Its name was Tropicalismo, a movement that would revolutionise Brazilian music. Caetano Veloso, his sister Maria Bethania, Gilberto Gil, Gal Costa and Tom Zé, all Bahianos, surfed the crest of a full moon tide that flooded Brazil's traditional and popular music with rock elements, experimentation and mutation. The Tropicalistos were talented, confrontational and controversial, antagonising both the right, that considered the movement radical and dangerous, and the students of the left who saw it as the contamination of Brazilian culture by commercial American music. When Caetano performed his song 'É Proibido Proibir' (It is Forbidden to Forbid), he was pelted with eggs and fruit. Dare to differ from long held expectations! It recalls the abuse of Bob Dylan when he swapped an acoustic guitar for an electric one, or Stravinksy whose 'Rites of Spring' performance in Paris caused a near-riot.

In 1964 the military overthrew the democratic government in Brazil and the generals did not like this music either. Caetano and Gilberto Gil, who have remained close friends and collaborators for life, were jailed for three months, then placed under house arrest. Eventually the two musicians were forced into exile and went to live in London, at a time of Pink Floyd and Carnaby street. When they returned to Brazil in 1972 their careers went stellar.

Choosing one album only of Caetano Veloso is proving a difficult task. A prolific songwriter and superb singer, he offers romantic bossa, dance and carnival music, celebrates the African culture of Bahia, recites political poetry, explores avant-garde, croons American standards in English, honours Cuban writers in Spanish and Italian composers in Italian, brings back the Brazilian songwriters of old, interprets Irving Berlin, the Beatles and Mercedes Sosa. Of his studio albums, *Livro* (*1997*) is a favourite, creative and innovative, with a sound of its own that I keep returning to.

But then I waver between two very different live albums. *Ommagio a Federico e Guiletta (1999)* is a tribute concert to Federico Fellini and his wife Guiletta. It is pared down and intimate. Caetano sings Italian songs from Fellini's films, originals and bossa novas. The divine cello of Jacques Morelenbaum, Caetano's finest collaborator, is featured prominently. Jacques is also the arranger and conductor of the second live disc: *Fina Estampa ão Vivo* (1995). From Spanish to Portuguese, from luscious orchestral arrangements of Cuban classics to Caetano solo with his guitar, from romance to politics, from tradition to epiphany. Breathtaking in its scope. If I have only room for one, I will take it. Unless I change my mind.

4. **INFINIMENT** BARCLAY *(2004)*
Jacques Brel

I have many favourite singer-songwriters, amongst them Bob Dylan, Bob Marley, Joni Mitchell, Caetano Veloso, Lennon and McCartney, Stevie Wonder, Hank Williams, Tom Waits, João Gilberto, Rufus Wainwright, George Brassens, Sting, Laura Marling, Hoagy Carmichael, Nick Drake, João Bosco, John Martyn and Randy Newman. The stellar repertoire of each of them would not fit into an apartment block. Each of them requires its own skyscraper in New York, Shangai or Dubai. But the Belgian artist Jacques Brel has bequeathed us his very own Taj Mahal, a couple of pyramids, as well as the Atomium outside of Brussels. His extensive body of work is well represented in this double CD collection. If I had an ark I would take it all with me.

5. THE SUN ESSENTIALS *CHARLY SNAJ 737 (2006)*
Jerry Lee Lewis

'Il faut bien que le corps exulte,' sings Jacques Brel ('La Chanson des Vieux Amants'). The body must exult itself. Jerry Lee Lewis is for these moments when, alone on my island, I want to let it all hang out. Every time children are rocking out at the front of the stage, cutting loose in wild abandon, unfettered and free, I recall the euphoric effect of being possessed by the beat. Even the little bodies of toddlers move with the groove. Early rock & roll was always more about joy and fun than about angst and fury. Let the spirit soar! Let the body exult! Jerry did it for me when I was fourteen, and young Jerry had just turned twenty-one and, whenever he drops by, he still puts my soul on fire and spins my stiff limbs in a dryer. Of all the rock and roll artists he was probably the most naturally gifted, an inimitable force of nature another could not compete with. Like Nina Simone, Jerry Lee Lewis was an interpreter who put his stamp on everything he did. On this fabulous four CD set a youthful Jerry sings effortlessly through 128 hillbilly, country songs and his better known flamboyant rock songs, pumping the boogie into his piano like bagpipes filled with gasoline. He was a geyser of talent. What he did with it over his long life is his tale to tell.

6. DUETS WITH THE SPANISH GUITAR. *CAPITOL P8406 (1958)*
Laurindo Almeida (guitar), Martin Ruderman (flute) and Salli Terri (soprano)

Yesterday, on International Women's Day, I went to a local exhibition of female artists. The artwork was inspired and the hula dancers were a treat. One of the artists invited me and some friends to a busy restaurant afterwards. But the food was poor and the music and chatter so loud that conversation was a burden. I came home depleted and went to bed. Then I dreamt that I was back in the Yassawa islands, where many years ago I had paused in a village of fishermen with my three-year-old son to lick my wounds before continuing our journey across the Pacific ocean.

The Yassawa islands are an archipelago of twenty volcanic and mountainous islands and islets north west of Lautoka. The Fijian government had closed these islands to land-based tourism and this would remain so for most of the 1980s. My dream had me drinking rum with two Papuan crew below the deck of a trawler when my old friend and travelling companion Stefaan van Ballaer walked through the cabin door with a wide grin and sat beside me. I couldn't believe it. Stefaan had died several years ago and here he was looking his handsome, rugged self, as if he had just stepped out of a Hugo Pratt comic. We both laughed and hugged and then the dream faded.

Stefaan, Leo Mason and I had travelled through Yugoslavia together when we were just out of high school. He had then proceeded to Brazil before the military junta took control in 1964. When he returned we spent many evenings together. I was awed by his stories and he introduced me to this wonderful album of guitarist Laurindo Almeida, featuring soprano Salli Terri and flautist Martin Ruderman. The pieces chosen range from European classical composers Chopin, Ravel, Desportes, Gossec and Faure to Brazil's own Villa-Lobos and folk songs. It is a rare musical heirloom from a previous lifetime, a period long before several interruptions caused me, repeatedly, to leave everything behind.

Soon after Stefaan's return I myself departed from my home town and I never saw my friend again. Years later, and out of the blue, I received a letter from him. He somehow had bought some recordings of mine and was making a film in Berlin. I can't remember where I was at the time, but I lost the letter and his address and however much I searched the internet in later years I could not find a trace of him.

How often had I thought of Stefaan when I lived in Brazil for seven years. Parissa and I went to perform several times in Berlin but I had no luck there either. Then, after a concert in Belgium, I met Leo again whom I had not seen since our Yugoslav trip and he gave me Stefaan's contact, but when I finally wrote I received a reply from his sorrowed widow, Sabine. Life can play tricks on us and time holds no prisoners. Stefaan is gone now. Sabine sent me a few photos from our Yugoslav adventure and that is all I have left, besides this album. Here's to my dear friend Stefaan. Thanks for your unexpected visit last night. It was long overdue.

7. HEJIRA *ASYLUM (1976)*
Joni Mitchell

I struggled to select a Joni Mitchell album to take on my journey, constantly lamenting the ones I would have to leave behind. Painfully, I pinned it down to two records: *Blue* of 1971 and *Hejira* of 1976. *Blue* is regarded as her finest, and I must agree. It is raw, honest, intimate and intense. 'At that period in my life, I had no personal defences' she explained. It is sad, poetic and sparse, the end of her folk days and the simple backing of guitar, piano and dulcimer. Her heart is open, her spirit vulnerable in every song. Is it a masterpiece? Yes.

Yet I picked *Hejira* as my desert island companion. Joni has grown. She is thirty-three. The end of a love affair has damaged her girly innocence. It is a darker record. She is hooked on cocaine and departs on a series of road trips, finding lovers along the way, their portraits painted in songs. Hejira is an Arabic word that refers to the move of Muhammed and his followers from Mecca to Medina many centuries ago. It means 'rupture'. And a rupture has taken place in her life. She questions love, loss and commitment, finds solace in romantic affairs while facing loneliness. The songs were written during these road trips, travelling in a car, and have the restless feeling of the 'fine lines of the freeway'. There are no piano songs this time. She could not take a piano on the road. The music is experimental and jazz-oriented, the beginning of a new phase. Jaco Pastorius's innovative fretless bass adds a singular flavour. The overall sound is consistent throughout and moody. It puts you in a certain frame of mind and that is why I am taking it with me.

But Joni is not defined by a single disk. Her musical journey has to be heard in its entirety. She is one of the most accomplished songwriters in the English language of the last century, a poet, painter and a composer who travelled far beyond what came before her. She contracted polio when she was nine years old. It weakened her left hand and she compensated by using alternative tunings, yet she became an ace guitarist, breaking new ground harmonically. She was a role model for musicians who imitated her, and for millions of women whom she inspired.

8. INDE DU NORD–LES HEURES ET LES SAISONS
OCARA OCR581615 (1989)
Lakshmi Shankar

I could have chosen many other classical Indian records, but this one has always left me with a peaceful heart. I still have a 10 stack CD player in my car and this disc seems to have found a permanent home there. I cannot take the car with me in my boat, but I will take Lakshmi.

9. THE DUSTY FOOT PHILOSOPHER *IM CULTURE* (2005)
K'Naan

I was a latecomer to the music of K'Naan. His song 'Waving Flag', an insistent Coca Cola commercial during the Fifa World Cup hosted in South Africa in 2010, had become a mega hit. It passed me by like a comet with the last goal kicked, but registered enough to be included in some performances as a contemporary gem I enjoyed singing. Two years later he jumped out at me from a 4CD box set dedicated to the 50th anniversary of Amnesty International, titled *Chimes of Freedom*. Among the seventy-three tracks of versions of Bob Dylan songs, rendered by luminaries such as Adele, Angelique Kidjo, Marianne Faithfull, Brian Ferry, Sting, Lucinda Williams, Patti Smith, Elvis Costello, Ziggy Marley, Joan Baez and the Kronos quartet, K'Naan's creative reinvention of Dylan's 'With God on our Side' was a standout. I wanted to hear more and bought some of his albums. I had *The Dusty Foot Philosopher* on my playlist when I worked out at the gym and in my car when touring. And still, I can't get enough of it.

K'naan is a Somali/Canadian rapper. His first name, Keynaan, means traveller in Somali and his name fitted his destiny. He was twelve years old when the civil war broke out in Mogadishu. Three of his friends were killed in one day, his brother arrested for blowing up a federal court, escaping the night before facing the firing squad. The situation became increasingly dangerous. His mother decided to take him to New York where his dad had gone to work as a taxi driver. Soon after, the family settled in Toronto, Canada. In his Somali youth he was attracted to song and poems, encouraged by his aunty Magool, a famed singer. In Toronto he learned to speak English, listened to hip hop and rap albums and adopted the lingo. But he had left a violent Mogadishu for a violent migrant neighbourhood in Toronto. Life in Canada too was a struggle. He was noted by Senegalese singer Youssou N'Dour who invited him to participate in his album *Building Bridges*, a project that enabled the twenty-three year old to tour the world. And so his career took off.

The Dusty Foot Philosopher was his first album. It fused poetry, Somali traditions and American hip hop and rap, recalled his childhood experiences in his war torn home country and the Canadian ghetto, and appealed for peace and an end to the bloodletting. He sings in Somali and English, bypassing the posturing of the American wannebe thugs of gangsta rap. He does not need to boast or act the tough guy. He has seen the world crumble around him. He is honest and eloquent. 'How come they only fix the bridge after somebody has fallen?' he asks. The production is fabulous, from the hand splashing of water of the opening track 'Wash it Down' to the last fade.

10. SOUNDS OF SUDAN *WORLD CIRCUIT WCD018 (1986)*
Abdel Gadir Salim, Abdel Aziz Mubarak and Mohamed Gubara

For many people, the world is delineated in a map of countries with colourful banners and guarded borders, but I do hear it as a map of musics, some deeply rooted in peoples and landscapes, others spilling across borders, journeying by sea or land with sailors or traders, to merge and invigorate other cultures. And when travelling yourself, you enter other soundscapes. And so it was how I became impassioned with the music of the Sudan. The hugely popular stars, Abdel Gadir Salim and Abdel Aziz Mubarak are featured on this disk without their wedding bands of saxophones, accordion, organ, electric guitar, violins, bass and drums but stripped down to the oud, the accordion and tablas while the third artist, Gubara, accompanies himself on the tambur (lyre). Ever since I crossed the Sudan from the Ugandan to the Egyptian border in the year 1968 I have been enamoured with them*.

Abdel Gadir Salim especially has been an inspiration and, eventually, I wrote a song in the Kordofan style. It took me eight years to write, forever strumming my guitar as if it was an oud and singing the refrain 'My Rose of Kordofan' long before I realised what the song was about. I recorded it on my album *All Alone*. In 2020 I received an unexpected Email.

'Good afternoon! I wanted to reach out regarding your song The Rose of Kordofan. My father who is a Sudanese singer recently came across this song and absolutely loved it! He plays the oud and loved how you were able to modify the guitar to sound just like it. He wanted to be able to play and sing along to the song but it was a little difficult to hear the lyrics in the video. Is there any way possible that you could make the lyrics available for this song? Thank you very much and I hope to hear back soon!
bashar amir

---

*The story of the journey is told in my book *Tarab. Travels with my guitar* – Transit Lounge Publishing (2008/2014)

When I sent the lyrics I received a reply from Bashar's father.

*'Good afternoon Carl, my name is Omar Banaga. My son, Bashar Amir, had recently emailed you regarding your song The Rose of Kordofan that I absolutely loved. I wanted to email you saying thank you for the lyrics as well as attaching an mp3 file of the song. I'd grown up in Kordofan and loved your song. I'd grown up as a singer joining a famous Sudanese singing group known as Igd ElGalad where we were able to tour most of Europe and share our music with the world. Most of our songs have a political backstory to them which is why I loved the song that much more. After I came to America in the late 90s I become more of a solo singer and was able to release my album in 2011 which translated to English would be called **If I had A Gun**. I attached the mp3 files of the songs if you'd like to give them a listen! I wanted to ask as well if you possibly had a note sheet for the song I could look at but all is well if not.*

P.S. I also remember your mentioning Abdel Aziz El Mubarak and wanted to let you know that he unfortunately passed away this year.
omar amir

I was thrilled of course. I don't often perform the seven minute long story song about a refugee's journey unless I have a good reason or the right audience. But to move a singer from Kordofan made me feel like someone who had composed a string quartet and received a phone call from Ludwig von Beethoven to tell him how much he loved the piece and could he, please, have a copy of the score. When searching through YouTube I came across some fabulous footage of Omar performing in Central Park, New York, accompanied by a large Sudanese band, or rather orchestra, with a violin section, saxophone, keys, electric guitars, rhythm instruments, bass and backup singers. From Kordofan to New York. Funky as! Check it out.

11. **OLHO DE PEIXE** *SELF-PRODUCED LS001 (1997))*
Lenine and Suzano

Olho de peixe, or fish eye, is a wart on the balls or heels of the feet caused by the papilloma virus. Why this wart was chosen for the title of this album I don't know, but I do know why it ended up in my prow sailing to my island beyond the blue yonder. It is Lenine's first and best album, the disc that launched him amongst the greatest singer-songwriters and guitarists of Brazil. It is an album of, mostly, voice, acoustic guitar and percussion. Lenine is from Recife, the capital of the state of Pernambuco in the northeast of the country. Marcos Suzano, his collaborator on percussion, is from Rio de Janeiro. Both cities face the Atlantic ocean. Close your eyes and you can feel an sea breeze blowing through the album. Lenine is an innovator. He inspires. He reinfused the power of roots at a time when popular Brazilian music was waylaid by commercial rock, pop and axe. He was almost forty when *Olho de Peixe* was released, but at the peak of his power. His percussive guitar playing is matched by Suzano's skill on the pandeiro (hand frame drum). His voice weaves around the rhythm. Together they create the perfect stew of Recife's north eastern tradition and Rio's modernity. The songs cover a broad spectrum. The driving 'Leão do Norte' pays homage to the state of Pernambuco by listing its cultural icons. 'Escrúpulo' is tough jazz/rock. 'O Ultimo Por do Sol' is an aching love song with beach sand between its toes. Every song on this disc is a killer.

12. AFRICAN PIANO—LIVE (1973)
Dollar Brand/Abdullah Ibrahim

This live album, recorded at the Jazzhus Montmartre, Copenhagen in 1969, as well as the studio album *Ancient Africa* were both released in 1973 the year I saw Abdullah Ibrahim at the Nimbin Aquarius Festival and were identical to the music I had heard then that gave me one of the most powerful tarab experiences in my life. This album has it all. Exuberance. Reflection. Ecstatic hymns. Hammered keys, driving bass grooves. Syncopation. Free improvisation. Constant excitement that demands to be sung; he often can be heard singing over the pounding chords. It demands to be danced to and cried with.

13. ONCE I WAS AN EAGLE *RIBBON MUSIC* (2013)
Laura Marling

> You should be gone beast
> Be gone from me
> Be gone from my mind at least
> Let the little lady be ('Take the night off')

These are the opening lines of Laura Marling's soul and heart-churning musical exorcism that unfurls over one hour and three minutes. *Eagle* is her fourth album, released when she was twenty-three, an impressive output that reminds one of a young Bob Dylan, or Buddy Holly. In an age of streaming singles, *Once I was an Eagle* makes a great case for the Art of the Album. Singles are short stories, albums can be novels. *Once I was an Eagle* is a concept album, a post-mortem of a failed love affair. It is not the first one of its kind. Joni Mitchell's *Blue*, Fleetwood Mac's *Rumours* and Bob Dylan's *Blood on the Tracks* all document the heartbreak, self-doubt, guilt and anger that tailgate a romantic car crash. Loss and sorrow are always our uninvited teachers. But, no rain, no rainbows. Crises have often provoked the finest art.

Eagle opens with a dazzling suite of four songs. The sixteen minute overture alone warrants a ticket to my desert island. It floored me, it nailed me down like cedar boards. The slow, low guitar notes; Marling's long vibrato, so close, as if I sat in a confession box; her lithe fingers running across the open C tuning of her guitar neck, like a spider scurrying towards its prey. I became so enamoured with it, I recorded a medley of three of its songs for my album *When Twilight Turns to Night*.

Whereas the first half of *Once I was an Eagle* deals with the agony of love gone wrong, the second half details the debris, the purging of the beast, the healing and the recovery of naivety. All tracks were recorded in the order they were written. Laura tracked her voice and guitar during a marathon session, in one single day. Multi-instrumentalist and producer Ethan Johns, tastefully added hand drums, piano and Hammond organ. There are hints of India, African drumming, pop and psychedelia, a lustre of strings that can make the album sound huge at times, but is it always Marling's story, her songs, her guitar. It is an ambitious accomplishment, literate, serene and ferocious. Intricacies and hidden marvels will reveal themselves with repeated listening.

14. HUAYNO – THE MUSIC OF PERU VOL 1—*DISCOS IEMPSA & ARHOORLIE (1989)*
Various artists

I have always loved folk music. It is essential music and deals with deep rooted human emotions and needs. Love, marriage, betrayal, survival, murder, harvest, morality, disaster, celebration, hardship, dance. It speaks the truth in many languages. There are no contractual clauses. It just exists. Even though it is recorded, it remains an oral tradition. Fragments of ancient poetry reappear, past verses keep popping up, melodies are recycled.

The Huayno music of the Andes is a fine example. It is the hillbilly music of the Andes.

With the advent of the phonograph recordings from the late 1920s on, the audience of Jimmy Rodgers and the Carter family exploded throughout the rural USA. Likewise, with the onset of recording in Lima in the late 1940s, the songs of the Huayno stars swept across Bolivia and Peru, birthing countless regional varieties. But all of them are instantly recognisable from that handclapped rhythm -a stressed first beat followed by two short ones– and the continual shifts from major to minor harmonies, from joy to sorrow. The rhythm soon gets under your skin. The shrill passion of the female singer, wrapped in a pleated skirt of many metres, the pollera, that bulges outward beneath embroidered underskirts, boots and bowler hat, her hand gripping the one microphone, her voice shooting arrows at your heart. The band huddled around her, a guitar, a mandolin or charango, an accordion, violin, harp or a trumpet.

'The music that makes my daddy cry,' my son Tashi called it. Huayno was all around us, when Tashi, then four years old, and I spent several months in the Altiplano of Bolivia and Peru*. We heard it in the village square and city arena, celebration and festival, blasting from market stalls selling copied cassette tapes to the campesinos (rural people, peasants). It cracked my heart open, it moved my pulse and made my eyes weep for all its sad wistfulness, its resilience, the hope and the tragedy.

For a while Huayno was the soundtrack of our life and the pathway of my soul. I identified with what it expressed. It gave me solace in a dark time. The year was 1981 and the jackboots of military dictatorships trampled all over South America. Pinochet had murdered Victor Jara, the nation's most revered song writer. A soldier cut off his hands, then machine-gunned him. The Brazilian military had jailed and forced its own bards, Caetano Veloso, Gilberto Gil and Chico Buarque into exile. In Argentina the generals had ordered opponents to be thrown from airplanes.

---

*The story is told in 'Tarab. Travels with my guitar' (2008/2014 Transit Lounge Publishing)

In Bolivia every city was under constant curfew. From 9 pm till 6 am. No nightlife, everyone rushing home, pedestrians bumping into each other, cars hooting, bus driver screaming, arguments and accidents. Out after dark meant arrest and, at the very least, to be held captive on the sports ground till dawn under the freezing Altiplano stars, guarded by soldiers. This is what happened to a guileless Japanese friend with no knowledge of Spanish. The atmosphere was oppressive. General Luis Garcia Meza had grabbed power in a violent coup. In a Time magazine in a Santiago hotel I had read about him being financed by the cocaine trade, and a man named Klaus Barbie, a former Gestapo chief, was in the news for recruiting European mercenaries. Meza's opponents were brutally tortured, disappeared by paramilitary gangs. There was a sense of dread in the cities.

I was a single dad, musician and traveller, living in cheap hotels and villages. We were keeping our heads down, but the curfews were stifling. While we lived in Cochabamba there was a coup attempt, the second one since we had arrived in Bolivia, and the curfew was shortened: from 6 pm till 6 am. There were tanks in the streets. No one fired, but we could not wait around and left the city swapping the soldiers for villagers in the Yunga mountains, farmers and fishermen on Lake Titicaca, the backbone of the long suffering people of the Altiplano and the coastal valleys, the Quechua and Aymara speakers. They too stuck to themselves and kept their heads down, as they had been doing for centuries, finding release in song and dance, in pisco or chicha. I scouted the markets for the stalls that taped copies of old discs, no longer available but still popular.

When we left South America, eight years later, with my guitar and the skin of my teeth, four cassette tapes came with me. Another four had been stolen from my backpack by Bolivian border guards who ordered me inside their office to have my passport stamped while their accomplices robbed our luggage outside. These four tapes, since transferred to CD, shall be smuggled onto my desert island raft.

15. SUN BEAR CONCERTS *ECM* (1978)
Keith Jarrett

While the concerts of Bremen and Lausanne (ECM 1973) triggered my adulation for Keith Jarrett, this ten LP set featuring 5 complete solo concerts of non-stop improvisations, recorded during Jarrett's November 1976 tour of Japan, is hard to beat. I could have chosen any of his solo albums, but the sheer volume and diversity of this package makes it a desert island favourite. If the port authorities catch me out and block my departure I will gratefully take the Bremen/Lausanne concerts instead.

16. YS *DRAG CITY* (2006)
Joanna Newsom

Joanna Newsom's voice and music are an acquired taste, so I am told. *Rolling Stone's* critic, Christian Hoard, found it hard to stomach, but perhaps he needs to give this album a couple more listens. Some are put off by the shrillness of her voice.

Others find the songs indulgent, too complex, too long. Indeed, there are only five songs on this album. The shortest one is over seven minutes, the longest almost seventeen. I have become enamoured with the complexity, the daring, the beauty of her orchestral harp, the quirkiness of her voice and the ambrosial orchestral arrangements of Van Dyke Parks, the composer and producer, known for his film scores and arrangement skills and his decades of work with Brian Wilson, Randy Newman, Harry Nilsson, Ry Cooder and so many others. The album is lush with so many strings, all recorded in analog on two twenty-four track tape recorders. It was marketed as neo-folk, but beside all these boxes the music industry might come up with, it is just interesting music that warrants many a listen. In my boat. Ahoy!

17. EN MANA KUOYO *REAL WORD* (1993)
Ayub Ogada

If heaven exists then Ayub Ogada now lives there, sitting on a throne of marshmallow clouds, playing his lyre for the angels flapping their wings with delight, while naked cherubs spin and swing, doves coo for joy and peacocks flaunt their iridescent plumage, blue and green. Ayub was born in Mombasa, Kenya. He belongs to the Luo people. His musical parents took him to the US, a trip that opened Ayub's ears to foreign sounds. He arrived in London in 1986 and survived from busking in metro stations and on the streets. Peter Gabriel, founder of Real World Records invited him to record for his label and to perform at the Womad Festival. His career took off; his music appeared on movie soundtracks. Ayub's breezy voice and his crystalline nyatiti, an eight-stringed lyre, will make your worries vanish and swell your soul with gladness. Its celestial soundtrack will also be mine on my desert island.

18. THE TRUTH (NY MARINA) *REAL WORLD* (1995)
The Justin Vali Trio

I brought back a collection of music from Madagascar, most of it very difficult to find. This wonderful selection from the Justin Vali trio offers a fine example of the choral skills characteristic of Malagasy music, the virtuosity of Justin Vali on the vahili, a bamboo harp with strings stretched around its cylindrical body, and the boxlike marovany. It features the awesome guitar mastery of Doudou and the expertise of Clement strumming the kabosy, a square string instrument with partial frets responsible for the fierce dance rhythms.

Justin is a Merina from the central highlands where the Indonesian ancestry is most obvious. Doudou is from Majunga, the main town of the Sakalava people who dominate on the West coast and originated from East Africa. Clement, or Clemrass, is from the southern port of Tulear, a town populated by the Vezo, Mahafaly, Antandroy and Masikoro. Tulear is a thousand kilometres south of the capital Antananarivo, and the heart of kabosy country with fierce music, as different from the courtly traditions of the Merina, as Carnatic music is differing from Dravidian traditions in India. The mixture on this album leans towards the Merina, at times hinting at a hymn or a minuet, then whipping up a storm.

I am a string player in awe. If you love charangos, cavaquinhos, ouds, koras, dulcimers, bouzoukis, santoors, veenas, mandolins, harps, banjos, ngonis, saz, violins and more, check out the musicians from Madagascar. And, for guitarists, try to figure out the tunings and dazzling technique of D'Gary. Other recommended albums are *A World out of Time* (Shanachie 1992) and *The Rough Guide to the Music of Madagascar* (Rough Guides 2005)

19. SAIL AWAY REPRISE (1972)
Randy Newman

In the year 1972 I did not own any records. All my belongings, except for my guitar, fitted into a backpack. I was in movement mode. And so, it took some time before I heard this awesome disc with every song on it, a gem. Randy Newman was not a household name. S*ail away* never made the Billboard Top 100. Randy was swimming against the currents and up the rapids like a salmon in a river of psychedelic rocks and endless guitar solos. The fickle gods of American music fashions had, temporarily, banned all orchestras. Gone the French horns, strings and oboes. And here comes Randy with these finely crafted songs, backed by his own orchestral arrangements. Unheard of! But do not confuse fashion with culture. Fashions vanish, culture remains. And popularity does not mean quality. The mastery of these songs and his creative talent were undeniable.

As a child Randy spent much time in New Orleans. His music has roots in the American South, his dial tuned to the past of Stephen Foster and Hoagy Carmichael and the present of Fats Domino and Ray Charles. Randy came from a family of movie score composers. Three of his uncles were celebrated Hollywood composers. It was in his blood. Before he himself recorded, his songs had already been successful for other artists. He was never a pop hitman, but provided others with hits. Randy Newman was the master songwriter, composer and arranger and would, in his long ongoing career, compose film scores for Hollywood Blockbusters like *Toy Story* and *Monsters*, and pick up countless Academy and Grammy Awards. If you like the art of songs, you are bound to be a fan like me.

'In America, you get food to eat Won't have to run through the jungle and scuff up your feet You just sing about Jesus, drink wine all day It's great to be an American' ('Sail Away')

Thus speaks the recruiter on a slave ship to his captives in this dark satire, set against a rapturous melody, that opens an album of piercing wit and gallows humour, tenderness and political/social commentary. Meet the celebrity whinger in 'Lonely at the Top', a song written for Frank Sinatra who was not enamoured with its irony; the reactionary redneck in 'Political Science' whose solution is to drop the big one now; the man inviting you to tea in small town America in 1903. The paranoid dream set to a jolly ragtime; a river on fire set to a sweeping melody; the farewell to his dying father that tears your heart apart; the smouldering striptease of 'You Can Leave Your Hat On'; and then the final sting in the tail: 'God's Song', a devastating portrait of a scornful God who mocks the stupidity of a humankind that worships him. All of this in thirty minutes and thirty one seconds. So little to stash in my boat, and yet so much. Pure gold.

20. REVOLVER *EMI* (1966)
The Beatles

There are many other discs that deserve to accompany me on my journey: John Martyn's *Solid Air*, Nick Drake's *Pink Moon*, Bob Dylan's *Blood on the Tracks*, *The Goldberg Variations* by Glenn Gould, Oumou Sangaré's *Mousolou*, Rufus Wainwright's *Want*, John Coltrane's *A Love Supreme*, *Will the Circle Be Unbroken* by The Nitty Gritty Dirt Band, Bill Frisell's *Disfarmer*, Tom Waits' *Mule Variations*, Stevie Wonder's *Songs in the Key of Life* come to mind. But, to satisfy my many moods, I wanted to choose a broad spectrum for my post-apocalyptic soundtracks. In the end I could not leave without a Beatles album. John, Paul, George and Ringo have accompanied, thrilled and inspired me for most of my life, as they have with music fans all the world. *Revolver* was especially significant to me. It was released during my last months of living in Mechelen. In the mould of the 1950s programmes of Radio Luxembourg I had captured in my grandfather's cigar box, the pirate station Radio Caroline now beamed the hits from a ship in the North Sea off the coast of Essex. The tracks of *Revolver* spun on high rotation all day long, while my niece Michou and I wallpapered my room on the second floor of my parents' house, soon to be my former home. It was my *Hejira*, my rupture, from Belgium, from Europe and from the soundtracks I had worn like a badge of honour. I would never sleep in that room again. We removed the album covers from the walls. I had collected them thanks to my uncle Fernand's music shop. I would never see my uncle again and the shop had disappeared when, years later, I returned for a visit. I emptied my drawers, stored my records and books in the attic. *Revolver* was my adieu. The window of the future was wide open. My destiny was calling. 'Tomorrow Never Knows'.

Scan the QR Code

If you have the Spotify app, you can listen to some of the music by scanning this QR code:

MADAGASCAR GLOSSARY

Antsa:	traditional rapping and clapping vocal style
Ariary:	Malagasy currency
Fady:	taboo
Famadihana:	reburial ceremony
Hotely:	small informal restaurant serving basic meals
Kabary:	the Merina poetic art of public speech
Kabosy:	square-boxed guitar with partial frets. Also called mandoliny or belamaky
Kalon 'Ny Fahiny:	old-time music from the 1920s and 30s
Katra or katsa:	shaker made from a tin filled with little stones, attached to a handle

MADAGASCAR GLOSSARY

Kilálaky:	popular music derived from the Bara zebu rustling songs
Lamba:	cotton or silken sarong, worn as a shawl or over skirts
Lina:	long-necked string instrument
Masonjoany:	face pack made from wood and water
Marovany:	large rectangular box-like instrument with strings on either side
Merina:	highland people of Madagascar, from predominantly East-Asian descent
Mora mora:	slowly, slowly
Ombiasy:	healer
Pirogue:	dugout canoe with an outrigger and a sail
Poopy pop:	teenage pop song style
Pousse-pousse:	rickshaw
Razana:	ancestors

Salegy:	electric danceband music in 6/8, originating from the Sakalava people
Sifaka:	type of lemur
Taxi brousse:	bush taxi
Tsapiky:	fiery electric dance music from Madagascar's southern regions
Vahila:	tubular zither made from bamboo with 21 strings, plucked with both hands
Vazaha:	foreigner
Veloma:	goodbye
Zebu charette:	the wooden-wheeled carts pulled by zebus that are Madagascar's traditional form of transport
Zebu:	the cattle of Madagascar, a national symbol. Zebu have wobbling humps on their backs and flaps of loose skin hanging beneath their throats. The flaps allow better heat regulation in arid areas; the humps store fat
Zoma:	market

ABOUT CARL CLEVES

Carl Cleves was born in Mechelen, a traditional Flemish town in Belgium. He graduated in his Belgian Law Studies and was offered a scholarship to study traditional African music with ethnomusicologist John Blacking in South Africa. This started off many years of travel throughout Africa, the Middle East, the Orient, the Pacific Region and South America, guitar in hand, acquiring musical skills and an endless supply of stories and songs. His adventurous life has included stints as an antelope trapper in Uganda, relief worker in cyclone struck India, foreign correspondent and ethnomusicologist in Africa and night club crooner in the South Pacific. While living in Brazil he became a popular singer and bandleader. He settled in Australia in 1972.

Besides a Phd in Law from Leuven University in Belgium and his Musicology degree in African studies from Witwatersrand University in South Africa, Cleves hold a Bachelor of Arts degree in Contemporary Composition (SCU), was a research fellow at the Federal University of Minas Gerais, Brazil, lectured in World Music at Southern Cross University and in Composition at the Northern Rivers Conservatorium. He speaks five languages.

He is the author of *Dancing with the Bones* and *Tarab: Travels with My Guitar*, an epic tale of high adventure and the search for musical ecstasy (TransitLounge.com.au), now in its second print edition. His six solo albums and six with

ABOUT CARL CLEVES

The Hottentots, co-founded with his wife Parissa Bouas, have won international praise and numerous awards, including Music OZ, NCEIA and Australian Songwriters Association Award for Best Australian lyricist. 'Songs both intimate and powerful'; 'a vision whimsical and wise'; a guitar style 'utterly captivating, pregnant with unexpected nuance'. He has toured internationally, records for the German Stockfish label and has appeared at all major Australian Folk festivals, including Woodford, Port Fairy and the National FF.

www.carlcleves.com
www.facebook.com/CarlCleves
www.youtube.com/carlcleves
contact: carl@carlcleves.com

TARAB. TRAVELS WITH MY GUITAR — TRANSIT LOUNGE PUBLISHING

'By any measure, Cleves deserves to be mentioned in the same breath as Thesiger, Burton and Newby. He is an astute observer, a passionate participant and a man prepared to undertake interesting, but never crazy, experiences. Cleves is a rarity. He is a true traveller in an age of holidaymakers and gawpers. He heads out to experience the world and reminds his readers that true travel is about sinking deeply into cultures and allowing unique ex- periences to change your life. The result is a journey that enriches Cleves and the reader.'
Bruce Elder – Sydney Morning Herald

'This is much more than a musician's memoir. It is a beautifully written and well-researched narrative revealing the philosophical, political and emotional journey of a man and his guitar traversing different cultures, extraordinary characters, near-death experiences, deep friendships, ill- health, a successful recording career, and perhaps the most enduring terrain of all, parenthood.'

'This is a book to curl up with and be transported to other places and other times. The intimate tone gives the reader the feeling of listening to the melodious lilt of a magical weaver of tales. The rich prose is filled with images that will stay with you long after the last page.'
Laurel Cohn – Byron Shire Echo

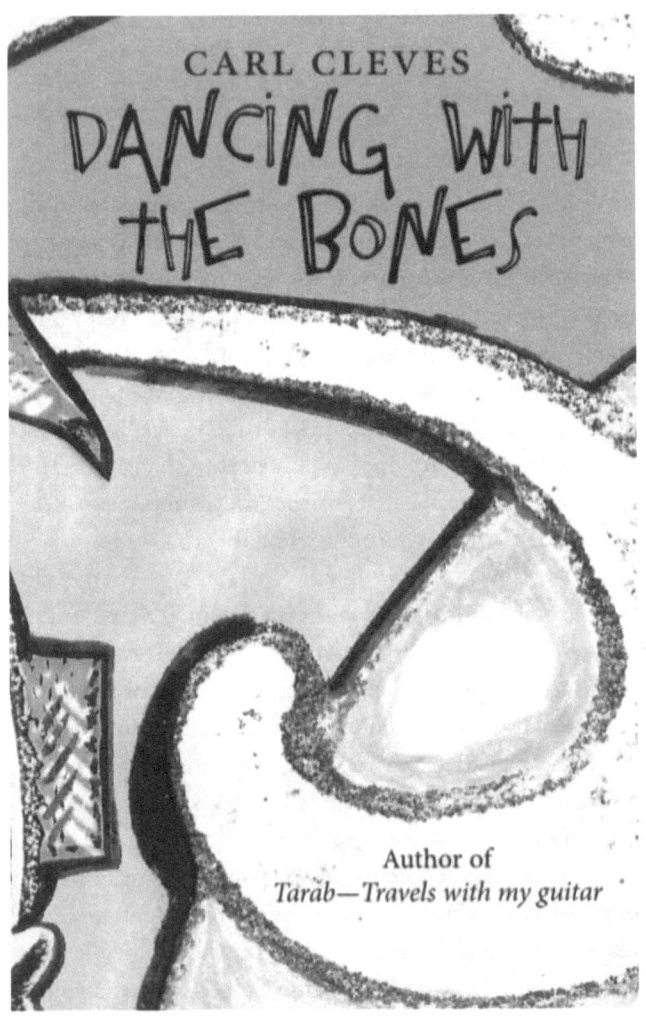

DANCING WITH THE BONES — INGRAMSPARK

'The book of my life has many pages missing. Some are frayed and furrowed with mould, others have suffered water damage, a washed-out cloud of ink dabbles". And I was hooked. What follows is an intimate invitation to witness Carl's boyhood in the Flemish town of Mechelen, through the last days and aftermath of World War 2. Carl writes with lyric sensitivity of the minutiae of family life and his ancestry.

Carl's musical manoeuvrings took him across Africa and India in the 60s and early 70s, without the blueprints we take for granted today. Eventually, Carl landed on the mid north coast of New South Wales, establishing a pioneering hippy life in the bush.

For seven years Carl and his son Tashi immersed themselves in the culture and diversity of Brazil. He and his band were much in demand and Carl achieved rock star status. I barely drew breath while reading these pages, so exotic was the imagery and intense the adventure. Yet again, as in *Tarab*, I marvelled at the fact that he is alive to tell the tale. And in fact, he nearly wasn't.

This is a memoir of the very best sort, a record of a life well lived, consciously, with wry intelligence and insight. It is also a love story, bridging family, the camaraderie of musicians, an unquenchable thirst for adventure and his inevitable meeting with the beautiful Parissa Bouas, musical collaborator and wife. "Her lyrebird voice instantly left a tattoo on his heart".

Of course, there is so much more to the narrative. You must read it for yourself. *Dancing with the Bones* is funny, it's moving, it's breathtaking, it's tender. I dare you not to love it.'
Jeni Caffin—ex-director Byron Writers Festival

DISCOGRAPHY

- *Before Twilight Turns to Night* 2018 (Australia)
- *Haloes round the Moon* 2014 (Germany—with Parissa Bouas—Stockfisch Records)
- *The House is Empty* 2012 (Australia)
- *Out of Australia 2010* (Germany—with Parissa Bouas—Stockfisch Records)
- *Tarab* 2008 (Australia)
- *All Alone* 2007 (Australia)
- *Turn Back The Tide* 2004 (Australia with The Hottentots)
- *Graceful* 2001 (Australia with The Hottentots)
- *The Voice of Your Heart* 1998 (Australia with The Hottentot Party)
- *A Small World* 1994 (Australia with The Hottentot Party)
- *Love is a Phantom* 1987 (Brazil)
- *African Lion* 1984 (Brazil)
- *Come Enter my World* 1966 (Germany)

REVIEWS

- 'The missing link to the classic UK folk scene from the 1960s.' *Folkworld*
- 'A real feast for the ears.' *Alternative Music Press*
- 'Amazing songs. An original variation on folk and world music.'
- *Sydney Morning herald, Bruce Elder*
- 'Carl never ever tries to sound like anybody else. He has managed to absorb these other influences while retaining his own muse. An uncompromising artist with a personal vision that is both whimsical and wise and yet he's not averse to injecting a bit of hokey fun into the proceedings. His melodies are memorable and moving. Carl's acoustic guitar playing is utterly captivating and pregnant with unexpected nuance. In fact Carl is the only acoustic guitarist in Australia whose work I can detect after two note. His sound is that singular. Yet he never grandstands.'
- *Diaspora World Beat*

www.ingramcontent.com/pod-product-compliance
Lightning Source LLC
Chambersburg PA
CBHW022047290426
44109CB00014B/1018